THE
ACCIDENTAL
ENTREPRENEUR

THE
ACCIDENTAL
ENTREPRENEUR
THE **SURVIVOR** EDITION

JANINE ALLIS

WILEY

First published in 2020 by John Wiley & Sons Australia, Ltd
42 McDougall St, Milton Qld 4064

Office also in Melbourne

Typeset in Plantin Std 10.5/14 pt

© Allis Investments Pty Ltd 2020

The moral rights of the author have been asserted

ISBN: 978-0-730-38454-0

A catalogue record for this
book is available from the
National Library of Australia

Cover design by Wiley

Disclaimer
The material in this publication is of the nature of general comment only,
and does not represent professional advice. It is not intended to provide
specific guidance for particular circumstances and it should not be relied
on as the basis for any decision to take action or not take action on any
matter which it covers. Readers should obtain professional advice where
appropriate, before making any such decision. To the maximum extent
permitted by law, the author and publisher disclaim all responsibility and
liability to any person, arising directly or indirectly from any person taking
or not taking action based on the information in this publication.

Contents

Acknowledgements

I have to start with my husband, Jeff, without whose passion, drive, support, encouragement and love I would not be the person I am today. My children, Samuel, Oliver, Riley and Tahlia, all who have sacrificed many things for their mother's dream. They are my true success story. My mother, Joan, who always is there when I need her. My girlfriend Amy, who spent hours of our yoga retreat editing and giving me suggestions for the book—not very Omm, but fun none the less. I am so lucky to be surrounded by the most amazing family and friends. That is true success.

Introduction

A few years ago I was playing cards with my gran, who at the time was 93. She was telling me what it was like to be a woman of the 1940s. She told me when World War II started most of the men left to fight, and she and her friends started working in an ammunition factory. It made me think about what an unusual time it must have been—when life as you know it suddenly turns upside down, your husband leaves you for five years and you have to survive by working in a factory. She started to make her own money and felt the freedom that this brings, only to be told to get 'back in her box' when the men came home. To think at that time she was not allowed to work or have a loan in her name seems unbelievable today.

In her time, women were not the bosses and certainly did not run businesses. In her mind, what man would even listen to a woman in the workforce? She constantly told my mother not to 'get above herself'. For her, a woman had very little to no real power, even in her own home. It took my gran years to understand that at Boost, I (her granddaughter, not her grandson-in-law) was running the business. She couldn't get her head around a woman boss—that was not what girls did in her day. 'Why would they even listen to Janine?' she would ask. Funny enough, it took a *Herald Sun* article for her to believe that I had actually started Boost (clearly only what you read in the paper is true). This wasn't popular belief from 100 years ago; this was my gran, only two generations away. Thankfully times have changed.

For me, life is a marathon, not a sprint. Mind you, it took me years to realise this. When I was younger I wanted everything now. (Sound familiar?) I did not have a patient bone in my body. I am getting better at this, as I love the journey that I am on and appreciate every day.

If you are picking up this book for the first time, here is what you are in for…

The first thing is that you will not be blown away by my literary skills. Like singing and painting, I have no talent in this area. But what you will read is my honest account, warts and all, of my journey to date. I go into detail about the craziest thing I ever said 'yes' to, which was *Survivor*, and, finally, I share with you all the things I wish I had known before I went into business.

The great thing about getting older (because there are a lot of negatives and you have to see the positives) is that you get to embrace who you are, as you see all aspects of your journey. What I hope is that people see that it's okay to not get everything right in life. You don't always have to be happy with the decisions that you make. And, yes, you are very dumb when you are younger but, if you're lucky, this enables you to have adventures that you wouldn't have had otherwise—because you aren't as stupid as when you did all those crazy, mad things!

Often people are afraid to make mistakes—they live a life half-lived because of it. This story is my journey—from an ordinary girl raised in the 'burbs, to marrying my soulmate Jeff, starting Boost Juice and Retail Zoo, becoming a Shark on the TV show *Shark Tank* and learning to 'survive' on *Survivor*.

For all those people who have given me feedback on the first and second editions of this book—thank you! I was surprised and delighted by the impact that this book has made on people's businesses and lives. I'm happy to say that the book is a bestseller; my English teacher from high school will honestly never believe it!

What is different in this book is it brings my story, and the story of Boost, into the present day—including some of the experiences I've had on *Shark Tank* and *Survivor*. This book is full of my lessons; these are the heart of what I believe you need to do to be a success in business and life. Success is not just money in the bank: it's having your family around you, playing cards or just enjoying each other's company. I learned this lesson along the way, sometimes the hard way. Whether you never want to start a business, or you have started down that crazy business road—maybe you are in start-up stage, perhaps growing like a weed, thinking about expanding into new territories, or even if your business is still just a great idea—there's something here for you. No matter where you are on your journey, it's always helpful to be reminded of the simple things that can make all the difference in helping you become a success.

PART I
THE SURPRISE ENTREPRENEUR

When you ask successful businesspeople how they got started, they may tell you about the little businesses they started in primary school—the ingenious corner lemonade stand, the school chocolate-bar sales or the lawn-mowing service employing other 12-year-olds. The types of businesses that led these overachievers to climb that first rung on the ladder to success. Sales charts, forecasts and ROI (return on investment) calculations lined the walls of these kids' bedrooms like posters of Andy Gibb lined mine. The entrepreneurial spirit seems to be part of their DNA.

My story is drastically different. You could say that my entrepreneurial spirit was … umm—dormant. Okay, it was non-existent. To be honest, if you'd asked me what an *entrepreneur* was in primary school, I may have thought it had something to do with food and would have had no idea how to spell it. (Actually, I still struggle with spelling that word.) It was 20 years after primary school that foreign entrepreneurial DNA somehow began to morph my behaviour.

During the 20 years pre-DNA takeover, I travelled around the United States, Europe, and parts of Asia and Australia. I had 30 jobs, got fired from some, moved on to others, made money, lost more, met the wrong man, had a beautiful baby boy and met my soulmate. What I didn't realise at the time was all the lessons and tools I was picking up with each triumph and pitfall. Each piece of my journey was enabling me to have the strength to take a tiny idea and turn it into a passion.

Of course, I don't really think having the skills to become a successful entrepreneur literally needs to be part of your DNA. I also don't believe there is a cookie-cutter process for success, or that success has to be hard or come easy. What I have attempted to do in the following chapters is to share with you my journey; it has many ups and equally as many downs. If someone had done the same for me, perhaps the learning curve would have been less bumpy. This is a short, honest glimpse into my archives so that you can see I'm human, just like you. I too trip over the kids' toys, go to work with my children's fears and problems running through my head, laugh, cry, make mistakes, learn from them and try to grow.

I hope that you take something from the following and follow your dreams.

1
THE SCENIC ROUTE TO BOOST

Growing up, I was a typical suburban kid. My passion was netball and I spent as much time as possible outside throwing a ball at the brick wall in our garden. After leaving technical college, my first job was in advertising—during the 1980s (think shoulder pads, big hair and liquid lunches)—and I even gave modelling a go. Sensing there was more to life, I worked three jobs to save for a travelling adventure. Telling my mother I would be away for three months, I set off—returning six years later with a two-year-old.

Just a simple girl from a simple world

I once read a book that suggested we actually 'pick' our parents. If that's the case, I picked the quintessential 'Aussie Mum and Dad'. Mum stayed home and Dad made the bacon. Dad worked for Fibremakers, a carpet-making company, in a middle management position. His aim was to move up the corporate ladder during the week and enjoy his time off on the weekends.

I'm the youngest of their four kids, born in Knoxfield, about 30 kilometres east of the Melbourne CBD. Back in the 1970s, the suburb was semirural. Our home was a tiny green weatherboard house—only 10 squares—but it was set on a quarter-acre block of land that had previously been an orchard. It was full of fruit trees, with an abundance of fruit every year (which could have had something to do with my brother needing to manually pump the septic tank every day). Uhmm...perhaps the love of fruit started here? We were outside children by necessity. Weekends were spent at the football oval for my brother, Greg, or the netball courts for my sisters and me. Our family was obsessed with sport. Netball was the one thing I was truly interested in during those years. I played and trained six days a week (even as an adult, I played netball until I stumbled into yoga at 41). Okay—healthy living and a bit of obsessiveness started to shine through during my childhood, but the availability of fruit and overachieving netball skills do not a businesswoman make.

My childhood was relatively uneventful; my siblings and I were much loved, and it was a stable upbringing. Life was simple, with not too much money being left over after the expenses were paid, so everything we did have was appreciated. I remember as a child the joy of seeing black-and-white television for the first time. I also remember going to the movies and watching that huge man on a horse, telling everyone how good for you it was to smoke Alpine cigarettes—as opposed to the other horrible, unhealthy cigarettes. I wasn't sold on the habit of smoking but, on the big movie screen, I did notice the vibrant green of the grass, so when I returned to the black-and-white television, I made a point of telling my whole family what colours we were missing.

Holidays were eight-hour road trips to Robe in South Australia, in a car without air conditioning or seatbelts. For Christmas one year, I got a bike that was second-hand with a damaged seat. Mum told me Santa had damaged it on the way down the chimney and, of course, I believed every word because I knew Santa existed. Looking back at my childhood, my memories are happy ones; my parents ensured we never felt like we missed out.

Even though my parents were encouraging of anything and everything we did, their aspirations for my siblings and me were minimal. Neither thought that someday we would own our own business, become a lawyer or even a doctor. This had nothing to do with not believing in us, and everything to do with expectations and our environment. My parents sent me to Knox Secondary College for two reasons: it was close to home and it had a business course. Okay, it was more of a typing course... In our neighbourhood, you completed your Leaving Certificate and then you got a really good job as a secretary, preferably in a bank. My school only went to year 11; my parents had no expectations that I would go to university. In fact, it was never discussed. Being the youngest, I could slip through the cracks. I was never the class clown or class dunce; I was smack in the middle—Miss Average. I never pushed myself too hard and rarely did my homework. How is that for dormant entrepreneurial DNA? I seemed to be always thinking, *What is the point to all of this?* In contrast, my older sisters, Rae and Lisa, were diligent, smart students. Not seeming to match them in potential or politeness, I was a bitter disappointment to the teachers who had taught my sisters prior to me.

My school was a technical college, focusing on practical skills like woodwork, typing, basic bookkeeping, graphics and metal work. As a result, I can type, build a solid birdhouse and do basic drafting, and I'm very handy with a soldering iron. But don't ask me the capital of Azerbaijan or where the country is located on a map!

My childhood was loving, yet simple. I was happy, but somewhere buried deep within, I knew there was a bigger point to this, that there was more to life.

At the age of 16 years and 10 months, I left tech school and could type 100 words per minute. At the time, I didn't realise that this was probably the most useful skill I had learned; everyone on earth was about to switch to computers. I could also handle very basic bookkeeping, which would serve me well later when Boost was without a CFO. The technical drawing class came in handy when building the birdhouse, but also when designing the first Boost Juice stores. You never know what subjects are going to be helpful in the future.

When I left school, my mother made me sit for the Commonwealth Bank test so I could get a job at the bank. She thought working in a bank would be the perfect job for me; I could think of nothing worse. My parents' plan for me was to finish school, get a good stable job, marry well, have lots of babies and live happily ever after. God forbid you not having a child by the time you were 21 (this was Mum's expiration date for starting a family). All I wanted was an adventure. But, to please Mum, I attended the Commonwealth Bank test to see if I could get a job. I doodled my way through the test and I didn't get the job (surprise, surprise).

I would like to be able to say that it was during this time that a wise teacher saw the flicker of an entrepreneurial spirit in me and encouraged me to think higher, but I would be making it up. My childhood was loving, yet simple. I was happy, but somewhere buried deep within, I knew there was a bigger point to this, that there was more to life. I just needed to figure out *where and what* more was.

First job, bad hair and many lessons

After turning my back on a safe bank job, I managed to get a job in advertising. My sister Rae was working for a huge ad agency at the time and she recommended I go to the employment agency she used to get her job. In I went, even though I had absolutely no experience. The woman I met with told me she thought she had the perfect job, and with a quick phone call she'd arranged an interview, telling my future boss I was a 'freebie' for him and that she thought I would be perfect, even though I was a bit green. After a 10-minute interview, and answering the question on whether I made good coffee ('Absolutely!'), I got my first job.

I was a very junior, junior (did I mention I was junior?) media assistant at an advertising agency. Advertising in the 1980s was all about short skirts, bad hair and long boozy lunches. Each Friday, lunch started at noon and ended at 5 pm. For a while, the fun in advertising significantly outweighed the boredom of my first job. (And it was a very dull job, mostly just typing little numbers into little squares, which, to be honest, after many liquid lunches, was a challenge.)

The ad agency was very advanced and had some nifty devices to help me out. They had these boxlike things called 'Apple computers' that allowed me to do a spell check (after coming from Knox Secondary College, I thought all my dreams had come true). Three months after I started, they also purchased a brand-new machine where you could insert a photo (or whatever) in one end, and it would print out on a similar machine somewhere else. (If it was a photo, it would print out a bit grainy, but if you looked really hard you could see what it was.) They called this machine a 'fax'. There was no internet, no mobile phones, and everything took ten times longer, but we all still managed to get everything we needed done.

My mother had rose-coloured glasses as far as her daughters were concerned and wanted us to do modelling. I happen to be a size 8 and five-foot-eight inches, which apparently was what you needed, so off I went to complete my modelling course at Suzan Johnston, like my sisters had before me. Twelve months into my new job at the agency, the people who ran the course called and asked if I wanted to audition for a job promoting Australian-made products. The promotion was to be government-funded and they wanted one girl from every state. Never one to die wondering, I went to the audition—and, to my surprise, was given the role of the Victorian model. I handed in my resignation to the advertising agency and off I went to Brisbane to start my very short-lived stab at modelling. After settling in to Brisbane and meeting all the girls from each state, we started our 'training'. Unfortunately, however, after about three weeks we heard the government had decided not to go ahead with the promotion—and I found myself out of a job.

Still, with the confidence I gained after getting the role, I thought, *Why not try modelling more seriously?* I had some photos taken and did the advertising rounds with my new photo book. It became fairly clear fairly quickly that my mother's view and reality did not quite match. Tall and thin I was; Elle Macpherson I was not. However, I did land the in-house modelling job at Adidas and made a *few* front covers—admittedly not the cover of *Vogue*; more like *Greyhound News* and *CB Action* magazine. In the end, modelling was not for me—a fact cemented after an appearance on *The Bert Newton Show*. I was modelling the new Olympic uniforms and went in the complete opposite direction to everyone else, tried to turn, tripped and fell. Not my finest moment and the end of a very short modelling career.

Next, it was back to the wheel of advertising for me with a job as an account coordinator. Multiple lessons were learned in this place. One senior male had octopus arms, which he used for big, long hugs and touches. When I complained to one of the bosses, I was told that I just had to put up with it (got to love the 1980s). The same male spent absolutely no time teaching me anything and kept everything regarding his work to himself. When he was sacked, I was given his accounts to run (Johnson Tiles and the SEC) and found myself way out of my depth. I tried my best to swim, but I simply did not have the experience or knowledge to do an effective job. In the end, the agency lost the accounts and I lost my job.

There I was—20 years old and jobless—when my friend Deborah asked me if I wanted to go travelling around the world with her. That was it. That was exactly what I wanted to do! I said I would join her, but the pull of a good party and buying new clothes meant I had very little money saved. When she packed her bags and took off without me, I knew that I had missed out. It was time to get serious: I wanted to see the world and live a life bigger than Boronia. I started to work at night for two nightclubs. One was called the Chevron. If you're from Melbourne and over the age of 40, you probably remember that this was the hippest place to be — and I most likely checked your ID. I was hired as 'The Door Bitch' (a term that was not always affectionate). The nightclub life was an eye-opener for a girl from the 'burbs. I saw all sorts of things: girls being taken out the back for a quickie, drugs and gangsters. I worked four nights a week at these clubs and got a job at a little advertising agency during the day. I was too busy working to spend any money; eventually, I had saved enough to start my travelling. During this period, I was so determined to earn money that most nights I worked until 2 am. I remember driving home thinking that if I drove in the centre lane, I might wake up before I hit anything. Young people can be dumb and, once again, I was no exception. I can only hope my own children are wiser than I was.

The adventure that was supposed to last three months

At 21, with a blue backpack, $6000, a plane ticket and a determined look, I set out on my own. I can still see Mum's bewildered face as I kissed her goodbye at the airport. To this day, she still complains that I didn't turn around to wave goodbye like all the rest of the travellers; my sights were firmly set on the future. I was off to Marin County, San Francisco, to work as a camp counsellor during the American spring and summer.

The camp was for children of different backgrounds, some with health challenges. Many were deaf and in one of the sessions all the children were blind. At the camp I taught the kids about trees and nature, and how to swim, make candles and light a camp fire. At the start of the camp I had to take the children through what to do in the event of a fire or an evacuation. I also explained what they needed to always have at the bottom of their bed — a blanket, shoes and a torch. I asked at the end if anyone had any questions. A blind child lifted her hand and asked what the torch was for. I said to see in the dark, which clearly would not help this particular child; she laughed her head off at this, as did the rest of the class. Obviously, they had played this joke before, but the experience was such a great learning curve for me on how people are people. Not only did I learn a bit of American Sign Language, but I also learned patience and appreciation for what I had as I watched these children with extreme physical challenges overcome daily obstacles.

When the camp ended, I travelled with some of the camp counsellors I had befriended. We travelled up and down the California coast, hiked the Grand Canyon, sat by Lake Tahoe and eventually ended up in New York. From there, we flew to London. I found the city a bit too depressing—grey skies, little houses and lots of rain. I contacted an agency that specialised in international travellers doing nanny jobs and quickly scored a job in Le Cateau-Cambrésis, a little village in France, about two hours from Paris. It was the birthplace of Matisse and the site of much fighting during World War I.

I arrived in the village and couldn't find anyone who spoke English (or at least chose to speak it to me), except the woman I worked for. She was, not to put too fine a point on it, a cow. I was hired to look after her three children and ended up in the basement doing all the ironing and most of the cleaning; I felt like Cinderella, without my Prince Charming in the distance. She wouldn't talk to me for days on end; at other times, she would shout at me for mispronouncing the little French I knew. The kids were lovely—or at least I think they were. They spoke no English and I no French; perhaps they actually said awful things to me. I will never know. Overall, it was a horrible situation, but at the time I couldn't see many alternatives. All I could think was that I should give it my best shot. And sticking with the job was good grounding in finding solutions to problems; when you travel you have to rely on your own resources.

I had been playing Cinderella for the evil French woman for a few months when a friend from Oz called me. She was visiting her father in Munich for two weeks and invited me to meet up with her there. I was so miserable in France, I jumped at the chance. Days later I was in Munich with the one line of German I knew, 'ein Weißbier, bitte' (which literally translates as 'one white beer, please'). A much-needed and well-used phrase when travelling through Germany. With the same friend, I travelled on to Denmark and that's where I spent my first Christmas away from home. In Australia, my family celebrates Christmas on Christmas Day; Mum makes a big Christmas lunch and we all sit around eating and opening presents. Denmark celebrates on Christmas Eve, so my Christmas lunch there was spent in a local hotel eating a sandwich and drinking a beer. Even the white Christmas didn't lighten my mood—I'd been travelling for nearly a year and I was starting to miss home.

After Denmark money was running low. My friend and I heard there was work in the Canary Islands selling timeshares, so we made our way to an island called Tenerife. Tenerife was a major tourist attraction for the English; its beaches had velvet-soft, black sand attributed to the local volcano, which not everybody thought was a good thing. (Two years before the time I was there, the council thought having white sand would help tourism and dumped 200 tonnes on the beaches. Within 48 hours, the white beaches turned back into the black sandy beaches they were meant to be.) My job on the island was to get tourists to visit the timeshare resorts that were popping up everywhere. One of the many downfalls to the job was that 'promoting' was considered illegal. 'Illegal' in the Canary Islands was a grey area as far as I could tell. As long as the police were making money off the promoters, they turned a blind eye to the dozen or so on each corner. This is how the system worked: a police officer would issue an 'on the spot fine' to the promoter (me), the promoter would give the police cash, the police would then give the promoter a receipt, the promoter would then take the receipt to their boss to be reimbursed for the 'fine'.

This all appeared to be a viable way to earn money, until my friend, who was now also my flatmate, revealed her dodgy side. She and an equally dodgy policeman decided she would purchase a receipt book off him. My flatmate then used the receipts to fraudulently claim reimbursement from the timeshare company. In addition to the scam, my flatmate used the money to buy drugs, thus leaving herself with no money to pay off the policeman for his part in the arrangement. My problem wasn't that I did anything wrong, it was that I was associated with her. I knew over a dozen English friends who were arrested and held without charge for simply being in the vicinity of a pub fight. (They had done their annual 'boys booze up' in the mountains and a fight broke out in one of the pubs. The police instructed all taxis to take anyone in the area who wanted to go to Playa de las Américas—where we lived—directly to jail. One of the lads was only 15.) In a country where corruption exists, association often means guilt; I was in as much hot water as my flatmate. I was facing the same fate as her if she didn't come up with the money 'owed' to the police.

The straw that broke the camel's back was when my flatmate asked me to leave the front door to our flat open because she had lost her key. I awoke at 2 am to find a six-foot-five security guard standing next to my bed complete with baton, handcuffs and a gun. One of his hands was heading under my sheet and the other was undoing his pants. You never know how you're going to react in these situations. Strangely, what went through my mind at that moment was not fear—it was pure fury! *Who does he think he is? How dare he touch me! Oh my God, is that a gun?*—these were the outraged thoughts that were running through my head. Making a split-second decision, I yelled, 'GET OUT!' To my surprise, he did. I kept yelling and he backed away saying something in Spanish as I stood at the front door. I slammed the door shut, returned to bed and slept. Thinking back, I can't believe that was my reaction. If asked, I would have assumed that I would be a dribbling mess at such a frighteningly close call. However, the next morning the full extent of what might have happened sank in.

After that night, with only a few days until my flatmate's debts were due to be paid back to the police, I decided it was time to leave. It was an easy decision to make, especially because my 15 English friends were still in jail with no chance of even seeing a judge. (They'd been there for three months by this stage.) This place was not a place where you wanted to get into trouble. My flatmate decided to come with me. After living in Tenerife for four months, we hitched a ride with friends on a catamaran heading for Portugal. Ten days later, we found ourselves in the Algarve in southern Portugal. I was funding both myself and my friend, who kept promising she would pay me back, but never did. In the Algarve we came across some fellow backpackers who had just returned from the south of France. They had been working on yachts for the rich and famous and their stories convinced me this seemed like the direction to head in, so I packed my bags and headed back to France, alone.

I am now in Antibes, France, with $40 to my name, no ticket home and $2000 in credit card debt. (I had cashed in my return airline ticket months ago.) Yet, interestingly, I wasn't the slightest bit concerned. Was it the arrogance of youth or perhaps that I knew I would figure it out? I'm not sure—but I do know, if it was today, I would be having heart palpitations. But in 1985, I just knew all would be fine.

The south of France was magical, complete with cobblestone lanes and old men playing *boules* in the parks. Restaurants and cafés spilt out onto the streets and dogs sat at tables like people, eating off china plates. The quays were full of large white palace-like boats, and here I was, off on another adventure.

At the local pub, an Englishman informed me there was a job on a boat called the *Deneb Star*, based in Villefranche-sur-Mer, near the border with Italy and a 20-minute train ride from Antibes. After a couple of phone calls (from a pay phone, remember mobile phones were not common yet), I got an interview. I was wearing the only nice outfit I had, which just happened to be a woollen jacket with a matching woollen mini skirt. It was summer and 30°C. Unbeknown to me, the train that I hopped on was an express train to Italy (and remember—this was before the days of the EU). With no passport and no fluency in Italian, I had to convince the Italian border guards that I simply needed to get back across the border to my appointment. Many hand gestures later, I was back on the train and off to my interview.

I arrived in the beautiful village of Villefranche-sur-Mer. I had a moment of bliss, soaking up the surroundings; then I realised I had an hour's walk in my woollens around a massive castle to the quay where the boat was berthed. The bliss turned to big drops of sweat and throbbing feet. Miraculously, I arrived on time, dripping in sweat from head to toe, to meet the captain. I'm pretty sure he didn't offer me the job because he felt sorry for me in my ridiculous attire and with my red, sweaty face. I believe it just may have been the tiny, white porky pie that came blurting out of my mouth: 'I have enormous yacht experience. I'm from Melbourne!' Lucky for me the internet as we know it and Facebook did not exist and he could not simply Google my name to check on my story. Suddenly, my money troubles were over. I now had accommodation, food and a job as head stewardess, all in one fell swoop. And after all, I *was* from Melbourne, and I had *seen* plenty of yachts. (Okay, maybe these were the first yachts I had seen in my life.)

The boat was 74 feet long. Think of a three-storey house with four bedrooms, a guest area and a further four bedrooms for crew. Now think of a cupboard—that's the cabin I shared with the other stewardess. The space in our cabin was about 1.5 × 2.5 metres and it was at the front of the yacht, so it was pointy in shape. It had a bunk bed about half the size of a normal single bed and the ceiling height was about 2 metres. And we had to share the tiniest wardrobe you have probably ever seen. Despite travelling in a cupboard, I was in heaven—I was on the French Riviera, cruising in a multimillion-dollar yacht. I had gone from dodging police, a potential rapist and a drug-addicted flatmate to floating in paradise.

Sex, drugs and rock 'n' roll

Six weeks after I started on the *Deneb Star*, David Bowie (yes, *the* David Bowie) bought the yacht. I was sailing the Mediterranean on the luxurious boat of a bona fide celebrity. Bowie was an amazing, down-to-earth, great bloke. He spent an enormous amount of time with the crew and we were very much part of his 'gang'. He took us to parties and was generous with his time. We cruised with him and many other rich and famous people to such events as the Cannes Film Festival and Monaco Grand Prix, and across the Atlantic to the Caribbean. We even stayed in his Bali-inspired house on Mustique Island in the West Indies.

David travelled with an entourage that included his financial advisor, Bruce Dunbar; his son, Joe; Joe's nanny; David's girlfriend, and a couple of others. Just to name-drop, here are a few passengers who came on board: Robin Williams, Mick Jagger, Eric Idle, Steve Martin and Michael Caine. This time in David's life was family time; there were actually no drunken parties, drugs or sex (although that doesn't include the fact that he sunbaked naked on the top of the yacht). There was, however, a lot of rock and roll. At the time, Bowie was starting a new band called Tin Machine, which meant a great deal of time was spent practising. During the day-to-day routine of life on the yacht, I would honestly forget that he was *the* David Bowie, although one day he was warming up with 'Space Oddity' and my mouth just dropped. I then said out loud, to no-one in particular, 'That is David Bowie!' (For the record, Bowie was a beautiful person who kept his feet on the ground. And if you want to know why Bowie has two differently coloured eyes, it's because he and his best friend were in a fight at school and the damaged eye was the result.) Years later when I heard of his death it saddened me to my core. Even though you would not classify us as friends, I always thought our paths would cross again. His friend David Puttnam and I got along like a house on fire and he often informed Bowie what I was up to. Unfortunately, it was not to be. He was an extraordinary man and the world is a worse place with him not in it.

Working on David's boat sounds glamorous, and at times it was, but it was also really hard work. We would have back-to-back charters for four months, which meant that you worked those months without a break. I needed to be available 24 hours a day and the job involved everything from cleaning silverware and the toilet to organising the helicopter to take guests out to dinner. While it was very glamorous to fall asleep in France and wake up in Monaco, the seasickness was not. At times you wished someone would throw you overboard. And I won't go into the gory details regarding a very large man who managed to destroy the toilet, leaving whatever had just left his body all over the walls and roof—*aargh*, not glamorous.

Some of the wealthiest people in the world hired the yacht, and I wasn't too sure what to expect from them when I first started. I knew from my upbringing that people with money were 'not us'. My gran experienced the Great Depression and worked as a cleaner—in her mind, if we got a job at Myer, we were doing exceptionally well. She believed we should never get above ourselves. (As I mentioned earlier, years later, when Boost started to get off the ground, she couldn't get her head around her granddaughter running the business. Gran was convinced that the part-time bookkeeper was the person I worked for—because who would listen to Janine?)

Meeting the rich and famous was great fun and a significant learning experience, especially about people. Most people who came on the yacht were lovely, like David Bowie; others thought they were superior to the rest of the human race.

On board, we had guests whose attitudes ranged from 'show us where the fridge is and leave us alone', to those who would send a boiled egg back because it was too hot. We once had a group of Americans on board and their kids were obnoxious. They thought they were better than everyone and treated all the staff like dirt. On the flip side, we had one of the wealthiest men in Kuwait as a guest, and his son was a lovely young man. The father asked me to type up a list of expenses for his son who was off to college in the United States. I was expecting to read that his son was allowed a fortune. To my surprise, his expenses were moderate. In fact, for the son to survive, he would have to get a part-time job.

Finding the resilient problem-solver within

When Janine's husband Jeff reflects on what characteristics Janine showed early on, the biggest one is being a great problem-solver. According to Jeff, 'she travelled around the world with tuppence in the bank, she was a mum at 25 and she didn't whinge — she just got on with it. She is a real can-doer.

'There is no doubt we were attracted to each other through our drive to succeed at whatever we were passionate about. Early in my life, I was passionate about assets, so I bought my first house at nineteen. Janine was passionate about travel, so she circumnavigated the world on a rock star's boat (slight exaggeration but within the realm of reality!).'

After two years and a great deal of fun and hard work, I left the *Deneb Star*. I was seeing the engineer on the yacht at the time and we both left to work on another yacht with him as captain (this yacht was anchored in Monaco). We purchased a property in Valbonne, a lovely village just outside of Antibes, paying way too much for the house because we had no idea what we were doing — and it didn't help that my French was far from perfect. A few months later, I found out that I was pregnant. Sadly, I realised that I wasn't in love with this engineer; I knew that he was not my future. Although the pregnancy was not planned, I gave it a couple of years to see if I could learn to love him. But he just was not 'the one', so we discussed it and I told him that it was time for my son and me to leave. It was as amicable a separation as you could possibly want. We had a beautiful friendship and he is a lovely man; he was just not my man.

In 1993, I turned to the first love of my life, my two-year-old son, Samuel, took his hand in mine and headed back to Australia. It took me 35 hours of travel and I had nothing but the clothes in our suitcases. Financially, the house we had purchased was not worth what we paid for it, leaving me without a cent to my name. My dear friends in France lent me the money to return to Australia. I felt like a failure — I was 27 years old and going home to live with my parents until I got myself back on my feet.

Landing back in Oz with a thud

Back in Australia after my travels, and feeling like a failure, it seemed the party was well and truly over. Finding a secure job and supporting my son was now my biggest priority, even if I had to finesse my CV a little to come up with relevant skills. Sink or swim? I swam like crazy.

Finding a secure job and supporting my son was now my biggest priority ... Sink or swim? I swam like crazy.

During my time on David Bowie's boat, I met a film producer named David Puttnam (referred to now as Lord David Puttnam; two of the many films he produced were *Chariots of Fire* and *Midnight Express*). At the time he was a director on the board of Village Roadshow. He told me that he knew Graham Burke at Village and that if I ever needed a job to contact him and he would set up an interview with Graham. Little did I know that Mr Burke was the CEO!

Regardless, I did get an interview with Graham and he was delightful—and I found myself with a job as a junior manager at Village Cinemas Knox City, not far from where I grew up. I did think it was strange that they didn't read my beautifully presented CV, or notice that I may have exaggerated the emphasis on my 'leadership' skills, but I found out later that Graham was simply doing David Puttnam a favour. I took the job happily and worked my butt off. I owed it to David Puttnam and Graham to prove that I was worth the punt. I always find that if someone gives me a chance, I feel extra pressure to do a great job, as it's a reflection upon the person who recommended me.

Even though I had never been a manager of anything before, as it turned out, I was good at it. At Village Cinemas Knox City, I worked with a small management team of three. I ran the marketing, a woman named Robyn headed up accounts and Sylvan was operational. Between us, the cinema did exceptionally well. We did so well that after six months I was transferred to run my own cinema in Frankston. That was a real eye-opener—the cinema was dark and smelly, and the curtains were infested with spiders. It was a challenge to say the least; completely unloved when I took it over, the cinema could not have been in worse shape. My first priority was to clean the place up; after that, there were bigger issues to tackle.

Spiders aside, one of the scariest aspects of the job was the accounting system. At the nice, new, shiny cinema I was used to, everything was automated. I could push a button and the accounts would magically appear. When I got to Frankston, I didn't even get a handover. I was presented with a key to the front door, a manual ledger and that was it — I had to just figure it out. Sink or swim? I decided to see it as a fantastic learning experience. Again, I got to work and within four months the cinema turned a profit for the first time in years; it was exhilarating.

The Frankston cinema was an excellent development ground for my marketing skills because I was so unconstrained there. I could try pretty much anything, and I did. I set up a movie club, sent a staff member out each week to put up as many posters as possible, used promotional material to create competitions and established loyalty programs. It doesn't sound too extraordinary now, but at the time no-one else was doing it, so it set us apart. It was like running my own small business in a regional area. Instead of seeking permission to do things, I simply went ahead and did them. There was no assistance, no manuals, no occupational health and safety policy—absolutely nothing. It was challenging but definitely rewarding.

I was, however, on a very minimal salary. I had recently bought a tiny house in Ringwood East (very tiny—it was built behind another house), borrowing money from the bank to do so. I did my sums and, on my salary, I could just afford the mortgage—and it would only take me a mere 25 years to pay off. After completing my budget, I discovered if I was very tight with my money, I could save $50 per month.

The house was close to my mum's house, so I could drop Samuel off in the morning and then make my way to work. With driving an hour each way to and from work, the time spent with my son during the week was a quick morning rush and a cuddle at night—thank goodness for weekends. So along with the long hours came the guilt. It was a new era for me. Gone was the freedom of letting life take me wherever it wanted. I was now responsible for another human being and the weight of this responsibility was never far from my thoughts.

Finding out what I'm made of

I'd worked for 14 months with Village in Australia when an opportunity arose in Singapore to assist in growing the cinemas there. With my three-year-old under my arm and a bewildered look again on my mother's face, I went to Singapore to start another adventure. When I returned home 12 months later, I was a basket case. I was burned out to a crisp. So what went wrong?

It turned out that the standard working week was six days and I worked between nine and 12 hours a day. Given my work schedule, one of the biggest challenges I faced was finding suitable care for Samuel during the day. After hearing horror stories about some of the local nannies (including one of them using her toes for a dummy!), I ended up ringing my cousin Rachel, who was 19 at the time. The company flew her over from Australia to be my son's nanny. Even with her there, I was still doing two jobs — working for Village and raising my son, Samuel, without the support of other extended family such as my mum.

I also hadn't done my research about my finances. I was so flattered by the opportunity, I didn't realise that I would be even more financially constrained living in Singapore than in Melbourne. The stress and the hours simply took their toll; I became an emotional wreck. Also, I wasn't prepared for the isolation I felt in Singapore. The expat community can be a wonderful support network, or it can make a place feel like the smallest town in the world. Everyone knows your business and feels they have a right to an opinion on you.

It was tough but, having said all that, at the same time it was exciting doing business in another country with all the differences in cultures. And Singapore taught me an enormous amount and was a great grounding for my future with Boost. Often in business and life the lessons you learn from your negative experiences have more of an impact than the positive experiences. Take, for example, my direct boss in Singapore, who was not as warm and welcoming as she could have been. Or my senior boss who, upon first meeting, said my shirt was inappropriate for the workplace. We were making massive improvements and increasing profit, yet his only comment was a derogatory one about my choice of clothing (which was, by the way, a business-style, sleeveless shirt). I vowed that day I would never judge people for what they wear but, rather, only by what they can deliver to the business. To this day you will see our employees walk around in shorts and T-shirts.

Through networking in Singapore I landed a job back in Melbourne, as a publicist with United International Pictures (UIP). I wanted a role where I wouldn't have to work nights and could have my weekends back to spend with Samuel. I'd never had a job in public relations — like all the jobs I'd had thus far, I wasn't qualified for this one either. However, my marketing background was strong and my portfolio of promotions work showed the UIP interviewers that I had the necessary skill set, even if I'd never had the title. So, one year after moving to Singapore, Samuel and I returned to Melbourne. This was a great time to be at UIP and, as on David Bowie's yacht, I was once again surrounded by movie stars. My overseas adventure had ended but a new one was about to begin.

2
NATURAL BORN WINNERS

I often reflect on my travelling years and look at what those years taught me later in life, and how what I learned helped me as a young businessperson. I think the first thing my travelling showed was a level of adventure and courage; an ability to give it a go and see where life takes me. Getting on that plane in the 1980s—when you could still light up a cigarette and some rows were simply marked as 'nonsmoking' (which clearly made sense ... not!)—and travelling to the other side of the world with no mobile phone or internet and snail mail as the only form of communication took a level of courage and adventure. Starting Boost was the same. Selling your home and putting everything on the line with no experience in running a business took that same sense of adventure (or naivety) and trust in the spirit of the journey.

Some of the experiences I mention in the book show that the young Janine needed to think on her feet and make quick decisions, aware that failure was not an option because the consequence in some circumstances was life and death. The same skills are required for businesspeople. You need courage, a bit of faith in your own ability, quick decisions and the power to stay at the problem until you find a solution. I would never have travelled if I knew the real dangers and some of the problems I was going to face. And I may not have started a business if I knew the struggles, sleepless nights and fear that came with having everything on the line. But then, how dull would life be? I have never had a desire to climb a huge mountain but I completely understand why you would want to: for the feeling of achievement, no matter how hard the journey can be.

A huge part of what makes a business succeed is the attitude of the person behind it. It's not about how many degrees they have or what blue chip companies they've worked for. It's about the hunger and the drive and the willingness to keep bouncing back from adversity and attacking the problem until you find a solution.

Doing *Shark Tank* was a bit like reliving my early days of Boost. The contestants were like all businesspeople in the early days of a venture. You have that confidence that the rigours of business have not quite knocked out of you yet. Every day brings a new challenge and it doesn't matter what education you have; it's like you're starting at kinder all over again. I'd never thought of myself as old before but I did feel it during some of the pitches. Seeing the naivety that some of the contestants had about their businesses was like going back in time to see myself when I started.

Winning people, not winning ideas

You often hear people say that they invest in people, not the product. The reason for this is that a great person can make an okay product good; a person who does not have that 'X factor', however, will not make a great idea a success.

I was a young person who was hungry and would not take no for an answer. Over time you realise that these people are rare; it's probably why four out of five businesses fail in the first five years. People say it gets too hard, and they're not prepared to throw everything at it. Trying to find similar people who are hungry, driven, positive, engaged and determined is not easy. What I look for is the ones who ask questions, take notes and are switched on to the answers, and you can just tell that the minute they leave the room, they'll be putting all your advice into action. That's the kind of person who can make it in business. I always do the book test. If you recommend a book to someone and they never read it then they don't really value your opinion and you're wasting your time mentoring them.

When I saw Kate from Be Fit Foods walk through the door during *Shark Tank*, I realised she had that spark I look for. Steve slammed her for not knowing her numbers and thought she was flippant but I saw determination and a passion for what she was doing. She mentioned that she had sales but the business was still brand new. The expertise Kate and her business partner Geoff have in the area make them a standout in the food delivery business. Geoff was a bariatric surgeon and Kate was a food and exercise scientist. They came up with a product that can help you lose on average five kilos in two weeks, just by eating the right food. Their product is also based on the findings from the CSIRO.

I decided to back her and purchased 25 per cent of the business. The business has had its ups and downs, but she is hungry and a quick learner.

After the show aired, their sales jumped from $50 000 per month to $500 000 per month.

Ideally, investors invest in people not product. The best product in the world will never see the light of day without the person behind it.

Attitude matters

A clever acronym I heard years ago describes a particular mentality, and it has since become a part of my professional vocabulary. This acronym is *VERB*, or Victim, Entitled, Rescued, Blame.

In life and in business, I don't like a VERB mentality. A *victim* thinks 'poor me' instead of finding a solution. They feel *entitled* to receive instead of driven to achieve and, when things go wrong, they wait to be *rescued* instead of finding a solution. Lastly, they *blame* others instead of taking responsibility.

The most destructive thing about a VERB mentality is that it places a person in a state of total powerlessness. Nothing is their fault; nothing is their responsibility; and they don't need to solve any problem because it's up to someone else to rescue them.

I don't want people who see themselves as victims—I don't want to hear 'poor me', or 'I will try'; I want to hear 'can do' and 'I will find a way'. In addition, there is no such thing as entitlement. I believe that people should be rewarded appropriately for what they do; I hate hearing someone say, 'That's not my job' or 'I don't get paid for that'. I also want people who find solutions rather than feel they need to be rescued. I want people to come to me with answers, not problems. Lastly, and this is a pet hate for me, I don't tolerate people who blame others. It's true we all do it at different times in our lives—and we wouldn't be human if we didn't—but don't be a serial offender.

The choice you can make is to instead use the SOAR approach, or *Solutions, Ownership, Accountability* and *Responsibility*. This approach is the opposite of VERB. If you use SOAR in everything you do, you will suddenly find things going your way.

You can find the solution to your problem; just stay with it. I love the quote, purportedly from Albert Einstein, 'It's not that I'm so smart, it's just that I stay with problems longer.'

Take ownership of everything in your life and business, and soon you will see the power it gives you. Accountability is there to remind you to fix no-one else and, finally, take responsibility for everything you do—if everything is your responsibility, you can fix it. I challenge you to SOAR—and find staff who SOAR with you—and see the difference.

Back yourself

We can all be VERBs from time to time, but my success came when I truly started to SOAR.

When Boost went from being very small in scale to a medium-sized concern, I found myself questioning whether I'd be able to manage the growth. I was worried that I'd had no formal business training or prior experience. I was starting to give myself excuses for doing things wrong; I was being a VERB. The fact that the expansion happened practically overnight, because Jeff had secured 28 sites with Westfield, didn't help! How did I overcome my concerns? To be honest it took time, but it was when I started to blame only myself for everything that happened that I felt I had the power to make all the changes that I needed to win. My superpower is that I make complicated things simple, using common sense, a clear vision and by getting the right advice from the right people. I realised these people weren't stupid—and if they backed me all the way, who was I to question their judgement? Or what it simply that I faked it until I made it? When you get older you realise that things are not as complicated as you think: it is mostly common sense, and no-one knew my business like I did. What I lacked in knowledge I made up in determination to find the answer.

Sometimes, questioning your own ability makes you work that much harder; having great people around you is an invaluable safety net. And it turned out the keys to running a business were not as complicated as I thought. If you simplify everything, are sensible when making decisions and look for the solution that exists for every problem, you'll go far.

Don't think I'm kidding myself here—when I started Boost Juice, I certainly didn't have the confidence that I have today. In the early days, I used Jeff as a crutch and, if anything was too hard or too confrontational, I would turn to him. Jeff, of course, had no issues with telling someone how it was.

For example, early on I invested over $5000 in a cash register for the new store; however, I soon discovered that it was an absolute lemon. The salesman I'd dealt with was a pig and basically told me that it was my bad luck. We had hardly any money and the $5000 would not be easily replaced, so I went for my fallback response: calling in Jeff. He called the salesman, who again said he was not refunding the money. So Jeff told him that he was sending over a man and he expected him to give this man the refund in full.

Jeff hung up the phone and put on a dark suit, his shoes with the biggest heels and some sunglasses, and went to the showroom for the money. He introduced himself as Jeff Jackson and said that he was there to collect. The salesman was clearly shaken and told Jeff he would have the money in 30 minutes. Jeff was waiting in his car when the phone rang—it was the salesman, who told Jeff that he was not impressed that he had sent in a thug to collect his money. Jeff calmly told him that Jeff Jackson was not leaving until he had the money in total. Needless to say, 'Jeff Jackson' had a full refund returned to me that afternoon.

Early on I was conscious that I hadn't gone to university, and believed that most professional people who I came across would know more than me. However, one thing I did have was a curious mind—I wanted to know more and I wanted to not have to rely on anyone but myself. The other thing I came to realise was that no-one could know my business like I did, so I shouldn't follow advice blindly.

I started asking more questions, not caring if the questions clearly showed how little I knew. I started questioning some of the documents and discovered that common sense and logic were really the main skills you needed in business. By asking questions, I also discovered how often so-called experts actually make mistakes, and that they didn't always know as much as I gave them credit for. Slowly, I weaned myself off Jeff and started to take on more of the difficult problems myself—even if, in my mind, I always had Jeff Jackson 'on ice' for another day. However, I'm happy to say that we never had to use Jeff Jackson again. It was my money that I was using, so I became a tough negotiator, making sure I was always over-prepared for every meeting. I'm not sure exactly when the change took place, but I do remember Jeff commenting that I wasn't using him as much anymore—in fact, I think he was a bit put out that his services as the 'tough guy' were no longer needed.

Education is important, but you should never lack confidence because of any formal education you feel you've missed out on. Education comes in all different forms, and people learn in dozens of different ways. I can confidently tell you that I know more about local and international trademarks than most lawyers—not because of a course, but by actually working out the issues in practice and learning along the way.

As you get older, you do get more comfortable in your skin. I still, to this day, listen more than I talk, and I will continue to ask and ask my questions until I believe I truly understand. Knowledge gives you confidence.

3

THE WINNING FORMULA

During my years at UIP, I was surrounded by movie stars, but my professional life took something of a backseat when it was overshadowed by a big shift in my personal life.

In 1995, I met Jeff Allis. We had been set up by my girlfriend Rachel, who arranged for us to meet at the Melbourne Skyshow. I would certainly not say it was love at first sight. Jeff was late and by the time he arrived I had somewhere else to be; it was one of those days. And I thought he had bad teeth and an attitude to match. Jeff remembers not liking the jeans I was wearing. He also thought I would have been better looking from the description Rachel gave him. (In all fairness, she told him I looked like Elle Macpherson! Jeff told me later, I was attractive, but no Elle. You will never die wondering what Jeff is thinking.) We said hello and went our separate ways. And that was it—or so I thought.

Working with movie stars and finding my soulmate

After the failed 'date' Rachel continued her campaign about how terrific she thought Jeff was. She kept talking about how great we would be together and, after about ten days, I caved in and called him. Jeff hadn't really impressed me, but my friend was nagging me and I figured I had nothing to lose. At the time, I was working on the promotion of the movie *Rob Roy* and Jeff was program director for Austereo Radio Network's Fox FM, so I rang him on the pretext of picking his brains about publicity opportunities. We arranged to go to dinner that week, but he rang the morning of our date and cancelled, telling me something about Adelaide and a sister giving birth. What was he thinking? I was this man's future, for heaven's sake! He didn't even reschedule when he returned. He was not exactly giving off keen signals, and I was wondering whether I should just move on. I have always believed in the idea of a soulmate and I did not intend to settle for anything less.

Jeff *finally* got around to ringing me back and rearranging our first date. And that's when things clicked. Although it was not love at first sight, it was love on first date. Conversation flowed, we laughed easily and we realised we both had the spirit of adventure. I remember thinking, *I really, really like this guy*. I'm not sure if I can call our getting together destiny, but a few dates later when we had our first kiss, the earth did move and I did see fireworks. Even today we talk about that first kiss.

Let me tell you about Jeff: he is a warrior, and he will succeed at all costs. If you were in battle in the Middle Ages, you would want him leading the charge. He has a fierce reputation in radio, with people like Kyle Sandilands calling him a 'radio god'. He features in many books, and within the radio world he was a programming genius, flipping Triple M from the bottom to the top in a few months. He coined the catchphrase 'rate or die', so you can imagine it was not all smooth sailing dating Jeff. When I was publicising the movie *Clueless*, starring Alicia Silverstone, she took a few of us and our partners out to dinner to say thank you. Alicia was touring and promoting the movie with her mum, and she was a real delight to be around. Arriving at Alicia's dinner, I could see that Jeff was in a 'Do I really have to be here?' mood as he began to down the champagne on offer quite quickly. We were taken to our seats and Jeff was seated next to Alicia, with me opposite him. Polite conversation started and all was going pretty well when Jeff turned to Alicia and asked her what other films she had been in. She politely told Jeff about her latest movie. Jeff was excited because he had seen it. I looked across at him thinking that his mood had improved and all would be fine. Unfortunately, we had not been dating that long and I didn't quite get the read right. Jeff told Alicia it was the worst movie he had ever seen and the only movie that he had ever walked out of! If a pin had dropped, we would have all heard it; the whole table fell silent. All heads turned quickly to Jeff. I jumped in and said, 'Oh, he didn't mean because of your acting' (uncomfortable giggle). 'It was the plot he didn't like.' I think it was a career-limiting dinner, to say the least.

Jeff, as program director at Austereo, was used to securing celebrities for promotions and programs, and so was also used to dealing with some of the very big egos that exist in radio. In other words, he should have known better. When I was on David Bowie's boat, I learned very early exactly how delicate the artist ego is. Once I said to David that I loved him in the 1983 movie *The Hunger*, telling him the make-up was amazing. He quickly turned, looked pointedly at me and said, 'It was, in fact, the acting that was convincing.' As he turned away, lesson number one, don't mess with an actor's ego, sunk in.

Seeming to have no idea that he had just insulted our generous hostess, Jeff continued to open his mouth and insert his foot. He candidly said he had not even seen her new movie *Clueless*. Alicia's mother turned to Jeff and politely, but in an ice-cold voice, said, 'You would not like it', and turned away. Needless to say, our discussion on the way home was not pleasant. Over time Jeff apologised for this night. And, like all understanding spouses, I bring this story up as much as possible, ensuring his punishment continues well into our marriage.

Another story I like to bring up is one that displays the 'whatever it takes' attitude Jeff had during his radio days. While he was working for Austereo's Fox FM, everyone there was at war with the rival station Triple M — it was a ratings war, and, in their minds, it truly was rate or die. Jeff and his colleague Sean had heard that Triple M was launching its new major promotion for the year and that all the top advertising agencies had been invited to the launch. Triple M was throwing a massive party with no expense spared, and with all the personalities, glitz and glamour that only the 1990s could provide.

Jeff and Sean knew they had to find out what Triple M was launching, so they asked a make-up artist at Channel 7 to make them look like advertising executives. Then, with their new moustaches (it was the 1990s), baggy suits and ponytails down their backs, they attended the launch party. Jeff recalls shaking hands and talking to archenemies, all while trying to keep a straight face. As soon as Triple M completed the presentation, Sean and Jeff snuck out through the back door, giggling like schoolgirls, drove to the Fox FM offices and formulated a plan to ruin Triple M's launch.

The Triple M promotion was based on a space theme, so Jeff and Sean worked through the night and created a promotion that was based around a sex in space theme. They then launched the promotion prior to Triple

M, meaning Triple M would look like a copycat if it went ahead with its promotion. The cost of Triple M's launch party was in vain, and the potential spend that it was hoping to receive never materialised. Needless to say, Jeff was not that popular when Triple M acquired Austereo. It could have been a career-limiting move, but he prevailed and ended up running both the Triple M and Austereo programming for the entire country.

Sean and Jeff were great mates and Sean was the best man at our wedding. Jeff and Sean were innovators in radio and rewrote the playbook on how radio works—those rules live strong today. Sean Pickwell died of cancer in October 2019, leaving the love of his life, Robin Bailey. He had so much more to achieve in his life. When my husband caught up with him two weeks before he passed, Sean shared his amazing views on life and death. Sean wrote an open letter that made the front page of *The Courier-Mail* on how he believed we should live our lives: with gratefulness and no regrets.

Over the first few years of our relationship, whenever people from Jeff's past told me they knew Jeff from his work in radio, I would hold my breath. What they said next could be really, really good or really, really bad. Either way, there was a general respect for this amazing man, who did achieve the unachievable in radio (more on this later).

Aside from a few hiccups and stories such as these, our relationship went from strength to strength, and Jeff and I had decided we would be together forever. However, I was still 'patiently' waiting for him to pop the question. Even fate sometimes needs a little nudge, so for several weeks I took Jeff to every romantic spot I could think of. Finally, it was the Yarra Valley and Domaine Chandon (Moët & Chandon's Australian winery) that did it. This was my last-ditch effort to 'set the scene'. I made sure he had a couple of courage drinks and then we went for a quiet walk, through the vineyard and down to the beautiful, blue lake at the bottom of the hill. We all sat to look at the white swans in the distance: Samuel, Jeff and me. Just when I was giving up all hope of him asking me and running out of ideas for romantic rendezvous, I turned to see Jeff on one knee. My heart jumped up into my throat as he asked me to marry him. He had with him a beautiful engagement ring to seal the deal (so had obviously cottoned on to my machinations). Once I said yes (surprise, surprise), Jeff turned to Samuel and asked him if he could be his dad and gave Samuel a ring. Jeff is a true romantic. I will always remember that day, even if I did 'help' to set the scene.

Things had moved quickly with Jeff. He had moved in with me six weeks after our first date, we were engaged after four months, married after eight months and I was pregnant with our son Oliver after 12 months.

Dormant DNA

Having learned an enormous amount at UIP about the power of PR, I left after two years to have our son Oliver and started to freelance. Six weeks after Oliver was born, I was doing the publicity to launch Triple M's new rock, sport and comedy format. (Triple M had bought Austereo Radio Network and the new format was Jeff's strategy to revive the failing station. Luckily they forgave him for his earlier indiscretion.) At the same time, I set up the marketing and publicity for a comedian who was touring with Stealth Productions—a business Jeff ran with his mate Sean. When I found Jeff, he unleashed that elusive entrepreneurial spirit within me; I never went back to work for someone else again.

When I found Jeff, he unleashed that elusive entrepreneurial spirit within me; I never went back to work for someone else again.

Releasing Janine's tenacity

According to Jeff, when they first married, Janine played the wonderful wife—happy to play second fiddle to Jeff's meteoric executive rise in the radio world. Janine was building their home, raising their boys, playing her netball and being a great wife. The family had fun—picnics and all the normal young-Aussie-family things, complete with a Magna station wagon, dog, cat and a house renovation.

Then, Jeff says, 'I ruined everything by trying to cash in on my wife's expertise in PR. In my little radio world we had just relaunched Triple M in Melbourne. I was given the task of resurrecting a station that was rock bottom of the ratings. I had hired every big name I could think of to launch a brand-new rock, sport and comedy format; for me, it was a make or break career move. The first rule I knew—surround yourself with the best. We had a great team on the air and now we just needed to get the word out. I thought,

(continued)

> ## Releasing Janine's tenacity (*cont'd*)
>
> *Hmmm . . . I'm married to the best PR person around (with a high care factor of me succeeding). Sure, she has just had a baby six weeks ago, but I'm sure she'll be fine.*
>
> 'Janine took the role with great relish and the station was everywhere — seriously. It was in the press and magazines for seven months — it was the most successful rebirth of a station in history. She showed me that real tenacity she became famous for. And now the beast was off the leash! Some women like to be stay-at-home mums, some work, some like both; there is no right or wrong. Janine needs the mix, and is a great and devoted mum when she is home. But to lock her in a house all day with toddlers? Not a chance.'

It was also during this time that Jeff and I tried our first joint business venture — a novelty book called *Love Cheques*. We had spotted a similar book in the United States, and we hoped we could convert the concept, put our own local slant on it and *bang!* have the next big thing on our hands.

The book contained cheques that you used as little gifts — an IOU message, that kind of thing. I thought *Love Cheques* would be the beginning and we would have *Kid Cheques*, *Mum Cheques*, *Dad Cheques* and so on. *Love Cheques* did okay, but the series I had dreamed of never materialised. We also published a book called *The Asian Mind Game*, by Chin-Ning Chu. We thought this was going to be another winner but, after a book tour and launch, there was very little to show for all our efforts. With two ventures under our belt and no money, we decided that publishing was not for us. We learned a lot and that's one thing Jeff and I have never been afraid of. So what if we've never tried it before? We'll learn.

Failure is a breeding ground for success

In 1999 we embarked on a joint venture with my ex-accountant, and I travelled to the United States to scope out the juice bar trend. I loved the category, was a big home-juicer and saw a huge opportunity for the concept in Australia.

Opening the first store in this joint venture was really exciting and I worked very hard on the launch, getting hands-on with every facet of the product and the business and learning along the way. But after many frustrating months we learned rule number one of business the hard way: the right partners are critical.

I was running around like a mad person trying to learn how the hell you start up a juice bar. Back then the internet of today was pretty nonexistent so that was no help—but I did it. Opening this first store was indeed the first time that I felt that 'you are a woman and clearly not capable' mentality. It was a bumpy ride with the initial partners, bumping heads over everything from red ceilings to how many blenders. I was, quite frankly, learning on the job but I was learning fast—sorting out the recipes, equipment, store set-up, et cetera. When we had our first meeting, after the first store had opened, the question was raised: 'Who is going to run the business going forward?' Someone around the table said, 'Well it would be Janine, of course.' The two other partners (an accountant and a lawyer) outwardly laughed. *Hmmm*, I thought, *you do know I am in the room right?* I left that day and decided that meeting was the last straw. I told Jeff 'we're out' and we took the money that we put in out and off we went.

Initially I was devastated: I had put thousands of hours of work, blood, sweat and tears and I felt it was all for nothing. But, after a very quick pity party, we realised that even though they had the shop, I had the IP all in my head, and the thousand or more hours of learning how to start a juice bar—because I did it. One thing I have learned in life is that more often than not, when something bad has happened to you, it turns out it was exactly what was meant to happen. This was certainly the case here.

Less than eight hours later, Boost was created.

It was the year 2000 and the GST had just been introduced; we were off and running. I started by purchasing a copy of QuickBooks, an off-the-shelf accounting package, and I then arranged to get a QuickBooks expert into my home to teach me how to use the bloody thing. I had no real idea about accounting, but I was determined to know all the technical aspects, so I would know my business inside and out.

After our ill-fated partnership, we were anxious to start again and not repeat any of the same mistakes—we would have full control over all decisions, including the site for the store. Jeff's 'real job' as program director for Austereo Radio Network took him interstate two nights a week. This enabled him to scope out possible sites in other states, and he found a site he wanted to explore on King William Street in the CBD of Adelaide. It was an old building that was heritage listed. He convinced his father, who lived in Adelaide, to sit at a table in front of the potential store and count the number of people who walked by and record specific details; he then broke this information into categories: men, women and age group. Happy with the flow, Jeff soon signed the lease and then called me with the news. This single act of signing a lease in a state that I did not live in truly shows the naivety that we had in starting a business. It ended up being an advantage—having the business in a different state forced me to work *on* the business instead of *in* it. But to be honest, I was so thrilled to get started and create Boost the way I knew it should be done that Jeff could have signed a lease on Mars.

I find often in the business world people get caught up in analysis paralysis and never actually get started. Sometimes you just have to jump in and start to learn on the job—this certainly worked for me.

PART II

GETTING YOUR SYSTEMS IN PLACE FOR WORLD DOMINATION

The first days of starting Boost were so exciting—this was our baby and we were about to see what other people thought of our juice and smoothie concept.

Having just opened a juice bar with our previous business partners, opening our first Boost store was not as daunting. I'd learned a lot along the way and knew what I wanted to do differently—now it was time to put all that knowledge into Boost.

4

GROWING LIKE A WEED

At the opening of our first Boost store, all I felt was excitement. It happened on King William Street in Adelaide at 11.15 am and, to my great delight and shock, over 50 people were waiting to come in. We had queues going out the door! With no marketing! (That was planned for later.) I could not get the smile off my face. I couldn't believe the number of people so I asked one of the customers how she'd heard about Boost and its grand opening.

She asked, 'What opening?' and then explained that there was a bomb scare next door and the building was evacuated, and ours was the only café on the street not affected!

I laughed so hard. A bomb scare is no laughing matter, but we had one of the strongest launches ever in our very first store!

Vision to fruition

Launching Boost was that little bit easier because I could build on my previous experience. I used most of the same suppliers, so I simply got the same terms I had already spent hours negotiating. I was having fun, doing the business the way I wanted to do it and not having to go through committees to get decisions made. Because of this, every process was so much easier, from designing uniforms to choosing product names to the creation of the products themselves.

We still made some mistakes in those very early days and continue to make mistakes. We worked on the logo and decided on the look and feel of the first store—but, I have to admit, we got the first store's look terribly wrong. The colours we chose were not what you see today—the store looked more like something the Adelaide Crows might choose instead of a vibrant juice bar. (This colour scheme was mostly Jeff's doing—but more on that later!) Jeff's negotiating of our first site was also a bit flawed. The store had no air conditioning in a state that regularly has days over 40 degrees. And because the building was heritage listed, we couldn't make any structural changes. So we spent the first summer running around getting portable air-conditioning units so that the smoothies and staff wouldn't melt.

For the next 12 months, I was forever on a plane to Adelaide (with three little kids at home, the youngest being under one). I visited Adelaide once a week, then less frequently as the business got up and running. Nine times out of 10, I took one of my children with me, while Jeff was at home with the others. I was very fortunate that my mum was also there to help out—she would come over to our house to look after the children. Without her consistent help, I just would not have been able to cope. I wanted it all—kids and a career. I made sure I got it, but had to work bloody hard for it and often got it all wrong.

We were also extremely lucky to find a great manager for that first store. A real diamond in the rough, Sharryn did not have any retail experience, but she had the passion and drive we needed and this was clear even when we interviewed her. When looking for a store manager, most people hire someone with an enormous amount of retail experience, and so I was often questioned why on earth I hired a person who had never worked a day in retail in her life—not to mention while I was living in another state. My reason was simple: she had that fire in her belly that we needed. She had determination and she understood what we wanted to achieve, and, like us, she did not have a history of bad retail habits. A sign of her determination emerged when she told us she was a champion speed water skier. You need enormous mental resilience and courage to be successful in her sport, and these were just the skills I was looking for. At 6 am, Sharryn and I were up promoting smoothies and wheatgrass at SAFM, the leading radio station in the state. We also collected email addresses to use to increase our brand awareness, and called members of this email list The VIBE (Very Important BoostiE) Club. Back then, this approach wasn't used that much so it was powerful, because people did not get a hundred marketing emails each day like they do now.

Young businesses are usually hungry for funds so cash is usually in short supply—and this was certainly true for us. This meant we were always looking for the most cost-effective option for everything. We needed to look at what resources we had available that might help, and that did not cost the earth. We were lucky that at Austereo Jeff used to get free CDs from the music companies, and these ended up becoming our prizes for joining The VIBE Club.

We did everything we could to get our brand out into the marketplace. But we also wanted to use The VIBE Club to create a sense of community around the brand. Every month, we would have great offers and competitions, as well as providing health and fitness tips, and this continued as our brand expanded. And I was involved at every level—I personally typed our first 10 000 VIBE Club names into the database.

When you're starting something from thin air, you have to oversee every little detail: from the distance the blenders should be apart (so they don't blow up) to making certain the managers have a checklist. This kind of attention to detail was not Jeff's strength—it was mine. I was in my element but I still felt a tremendous amount of pressure at a very micro level to get everything perfect.

My biggest mission was 'the customer experience' and nothing was too much trouble. If the customers did not like a drink, we would change it. I wanted Boost to be the business other businesses strived to be regarding customer service. My dilemma was how to find out if we were not delivering on the customer experience, so we could then change what we were doing. We needed the right mechanisms in place, so we started with the idea of detailing on every store wall the experience the customer should have. We called this the Boost Guarantee—every store still has one, and it covers everything from the kind of ingredients we use, and our focus on friendly service and healthy living, to giving people a reason to smile.

My biggest mission was 'the customer experience' and nothing was too much trouble ... I wanted Boost to be the business other businesses strived to be regarding customer service.

We then invited people to tell me, personally, if we did not get it right. This gave us a chance to change a negative customer experience into a positive one. Aussies generally are not big on complaining, preferring just to walk away, but I invited them to do so and made it easy for them, thus allowing us to find out how we were measuring up. With every single complaint, it became my personal challenge to convert that customer into a raving fan. I did it, every time—by thinking as a consumer and keeping it simple. At the end of the day, people know that things can and will go wrong. What made the difference? We acknowledged any mistakes, and then fixed the problem. Right a wrong—simple. My customer experience mission gave our customers a reason to choose Boost and still keeps them coming back today.

From the beginning, we were never going to be happy with just one Boost Juice store; we thought big from the start. Thinking bigger made us act bigger, and this influenced suppliers and landlords to believe in our vision, give us good prices and take us seriously. It turned out that starting the first store in Adelaide was brilliant. We were able to get the concept right without the eyes of the larger cities on us.

After the first store, I took total control of the brand look and feel. I realised the first store's design was terrible because I was using other people's views, mainly Jeff's. The new look for the brand actually originated from a massive picture of sliced tomatoes I saw in a store in Singapore. I know it may seem odd, but the picture was beautiful and it really showed the life essence of this fruit. We experimented with other fruits—I had our photographer cut oranges, lemons, watermelons and so on. He then stuck the images on glass and let sunlight come through. The effect was amazing—the simple beauty and life of the fruit was captured in the photos. We used these photos as the core of the design concept; we chose the colours from the fruit and the early stores all had three-metre images of sliced fruit all over them. The design was a winner—and, needless to say, Jeff will now openly tell you that he is not the one to talk to about design.

I gained many lessons from setting up our first Boost stores and over the following 12 months.

Showing stubborn persistence and gaining confidence

In the early days of starting Boost, Jeff describes Janine as a young woman with all the ability but no experience. Jeff says, 'With that came a lack of confidence in some areas, but she took the "Einstein approach", and just stayed with the problems until she figured them out. The personal confrontations with suppliers or shop fitters were difficult at first for her; I often got dragged in to make the hard phone call or appear at a face-to-face meeting. And, admittedly, being a self-obsessed radio guy, I no doubt had little knowledge of how hard the situation was for her—the obstacles she was overcoming or the day-to-day problems.

'Janine was scared, but at the same time she was relishing the challenge. I knew she couldn't fail, but doing so was her biggest fear (as it is with most young, driven people). I was busy with my "high-powered" radio position and not being overly supportive, and she was starting to build her own team of young, driven, motivated women that believed in her and her dream. Eventually the inevitable happened: Janine became more confident and busy, and I became less important and received fewer phone calls; I wasn't needed half as much as I would have liked. The tables had begun to turn.'

Making the decision to franchise

Jeff and I decided to franchise quite early, although at the time neither of us knew much about franchising or how it worked. Our vision was always to grow the brand and we realised we had a small window to do so before bigger players came into the marketplace. We just wouldn't be able to hire enough quality managers to expand that quickly—and that's where franchising offered us the solution we were looking for.

Through a friend of a friend we stumbled upon Rod Young, who was just opening a franchise advisory business after having worked in franchising and business his entire professional life. We were his very first clients in his new venture and he became a small shareholder in ours.

Our first meeting with Rod was before we had completed a full year of trading. I remember this because Rod explained we would need figures for a full 12 months before we could begin franchising. Even so, we were clear on our direction. It was 2001, and this would be the road we headed down.

Keep in mind, I was learning on the go and had three young boys at home; every day presented a new set of problems to solve. Thank heaven for my mother! Not long after we had made the decision to start franchising,

Jeff (who looked after leasing) came home one night with a smile like the Cheshire Cat. I knew that grin; it comes out when he has done something that he knows will freak me out—and he had! He had just signed a 28-store deal with Westfield, complete with a $5 million liability in our names! Like most early (okay, mid) thirtysomethings with a young family, we had no money. After a seven-second calculation, I knew the equity in our house was not worth one tenth of this figure. We needed to open 28 stores within 18 months and, at the time, we only had two stores open. This deadline didn't just give me a little kickstart; it exploded me into the world of franchising—without a parachute.

Despite my initial shock, franchising did work for us—massively. We had so many franchise enquiries we could barely manage the load. Fortuitously, we'd recently hired a very young head of human resources (HR), Jacinta Caithness. (At the time, we still worked out of our home and on her first day, Jacinta was greeted at the front door by Molly, our massive Great Dane. I could see in her eyes that she was wondering whether she should stick with the job or make a run for it. Thankfully she didn't run, and I immediately stopped letting Molly greet recruits.) While Jacinta started as our HR manager, she quickly became our franchise manager, and she did an amazing job recruiting the right people for our franchise businesses. On the leasing side, I also worked closely with Kristie Piniuta, a lawyer who would later come to work for Boost.

Solving every problem on the table

In 2002 Kristie was a new lawyer specialising in retail leasing, acting on behalf of tenants. Boost was meant to be her 'pet project', with four shops open and a few more expected that year as the company started franchising its concept. Things didn't quite work out like that, however—her 'pet client' opened 50 stores that year. Kristie says, 'I loved it! J [Janine] and I discussed leases not like they were just a legal document to get right, but rather as the basis for the success of a Boost business.'

Shortly after, Kristie was seconded to Boost's support centre and, she says, 'within one hour of that secondment I was asked to join the Boost team—and I jumped ship with enthusiasm. I felt alive and valued when I worked with Boost. Everyone was so engaged. It was fun and yet constructive—in 30 minutes, it seemed we could solve every problem on the table.'

To franchise or not to franchise ...

What to franchise? When to franchise? It seems that everyone with an idea is trying to franchise it these days. So how do you know if your idea is a good bet? When should you franchise? At Boost, we were very quick to franchise and, for us, it was definitely the right move. The speed of our growth was so rapid in the early days that franchising was the only viable option to maintain this growth momentum, and it worked well for our business model. But franchising isn't for everyone. Before you take that plunge, you should consider whether your business model is appropriate to your business.

The first thing I'd say is if you have a business that is only slightly profitable after royalties, do not franchise, because it will be a world of pain! Franchising only works if you have a proven profitable model that is transferable and has growth potential.

You need at least a year's worth of figures that are profitable. You also need to make sure that you're in possession of a full operations kit (a 'how-to' guide with tools, forms and information) so that everyone knows exactly what they're doing. And you need to be certain that your intellectual property rights and trademarks are set up and protected. And I'd recommend you hire a solid accountant and lawyer to ensure you get it right—once you know the rules, the process is not difficult.

Next, you need to be sure your business is a good franchise option. Work out if your concept is a profitable model that can be transferred to another location. I have a friend who's a naturopath, and she is so successful that she was considering franchising. Unfortunately, in her situation it's not possible—she is her business. If she could find 100 clones of herself to run the franchises, yes, it would work, but that's not going to happen! In my friend's case, she's now considering creating a product line instead. Remember—franchising may not be for you, but there are always other ways to expand your business.

Assuming your business is making money and is transferable, what are the benefits of franchising? For me, franchising has five enormous benefits:

1. *Market ownership:* If you have a good concept that's busting to grow, you need to claim your market—if you do not grow your

concept, someone else will! Don't let anyone steal your hard work right out from under you. Franchising allows you to expand your concept into new territories without having to physically be there yourself, because you get like-minded people involved in your business who also have ownership, and you know that they have the care factor to make the business work. You need to be first in the minds of your consumers. Without this advantage, growing a brand is difficult.

2. *People:* When you franchise, you expand your operation with passionate, like-minded owners who will work as hard as you do to build their own businesses as part of your network. The good franchises really tap into this great resource to grow their business.

3. *Capital:* Franchising allows you to grow your business with limited capital outlay.

4. *Marketing:* Franchises pool their resources so that they can market effectively as a group. Franchising is also a great way to get market penetration by opening lots of stores, which in itself is a great marketing tool.

5. *Buying power:* With mass orders come great savings. Many businesses need to get to a certain size before they are big enough to make decent money. With a franchise, even though you have one store, you leverage the group and you immediately have better buying power.

So if your business is straining to grow, do the sums. Franchising just might be the perfect solution for you. However, while franchising is often viewed as a golden ticket to retirement, it can be a nightmare.

Franchising comes with four major stings in the tail. These are:

1. *Set-up costs:* Legal costs and aspects such as preparing your training manuals and documenting your systems so you set your business up to franchise can cost in excess of $100 000. Of course, if you do it right, it is well worth the investment.

2. *High risk of litigation:* Whenever you are dealing with people and large amounts of money, even if you do everything right, you are still at risk of being sued. When all good intentions go wrong, for example, sometimes a franchisee can be losing money for many

reasons, but often they look for someone to blame, and often this is the franchisor. When I first started out, my lawyer said to me that the one thing that was guaranteed was that, sometime down the track, someone would sue me. If you ever go through this process, you will know there are no winners (other than the lawyers) and it is a world of pain.

3. *Systems pressure:* If you thought that running a business required you to have good systems and processes in place, well, multiply that pressure by 10 to get closer to the requirements once you franchise. The Franchise Code of Conduct needs to be followed, and you need systems for tracking sales, communication, marketing, HR (et cetera, et cetera). So your business needs to be in great shape before you franchise. You will need to continually invest in digital systems to keep your business robust.

4. *People:* While getting great people to deal with and share great ideas is a great positive (because nothing is better than being surrounded by dynamic, innovative people), the negative is that, because we are all human, you'll also likely have to deal with negative people who love the blame game. It is also very hard when, for whatever reason, the business does not work for them or perhaps they have a change in life, such as a divorce. You need to ride that path with them, understanding it can be very hard emotionally to run a franchise business.

So before you make the leap, consider carefully what kind of model your business is best suited to.

The Boost franchising method

I always felt that Boost was going to be big (which shows just how naive I was, and lacking in any true knowledge of what was involved to make this prediction a reality).

In the very early days, I hadn't considered how exactly I was going to create all these stores. I simply thought I'd have another and another and another... Unfortunately, as the brand expanded, I simply couldn't hire the high-quality people I needed as well as expand. I realised early that if we wanted to grow quickly, people in the company needed to have ownership—and there's nothing like having everything on the line to make a business work well. Enter franchising.

I'd never had anything to do with franchising, and didn't really understand how it worked. We met Rod Young, a franchise industry consultant, and approached him to advise us in setting up the Boost Juice franchise. I always think that if you're going to do something, you should do it right, and getting Rod on board to help us avoid some of the basic mistakes in franchising was a good thing for us in the early days—at the time, he was the best in the business.

Another important factor was getting the right franchise manager, which was Jacinta. I've always seen our franchise manager as the gatekeeper of the Boost Juice name. I imagine her standing in a knight outfit (with a very sharp sword) on a plank outside the Boost castle, and I know that she will not let the wrong people into the business (or *our* business, as she would say). We do not tolerate mediocrity. Believe it or not, the best decisions we have made involve the people who we did not hire!

For Boost Juice, franchising has been a wonderful way to get amazing people into our business and to create ownership in individual Boost stores. We call our franchisees 'Boost partners' and in a sense that's what they are. Franchisees pay Boost an ongoing royalty—a percentage of turnover—for the right to use our brand on a single store. They are buying into the brand and the support we give them. The statistics are very straightforward with regard to the success of running a business. In fact you are three times more likely to succeed in a good franchise business than starting on your own—BUT it does not guarantee success. It is still a lot of hard work and sacrifice, and getting all the bits and pieces right in order for it to actually work. If you want an investment, buy property or shares; a business is not that.

As the franchisor, we get two major benefits from the relationship. The first is growth of the brand. The second is the quality of the people you bring into your business to run the individual stores. Both the franchisor and franchisee have the same motivation to be successful, and both parties have everything on the line to make it work; this is a great motivator.

It's not easy to become a Boost franchisee. We are known within the franchising world as being incredibly selective—and we're proud of that. Our existing partners, in particular, love this reputation because they know that any new partner has undergone rigorous assessment. Our selection process for new partners (new franchisees) is one of the most robust and rigorous within our industry. Our dedicated franchising team receives over

400 enquiries a month; of these, one partner is likely to receive keys to their own store. We are fortunate to have an incredibly engaged partner group who have an appetite for further expansion and often snap up new Boost opportunities before they are available to the public.

When selecting a new partner, we are not prepared to settle for mediocrity; our process helps us to get the right people in our business, and ensure our partners are aligned to our values. Our brand is our greatest strength, so we do everything we can to protect it.

Shortly after a new partner has been approved to join our network, they will undertake a three-week intensive training program. This in-depth training program encompasses subjects relating to business management, operational excellence and the customer experience.

Consistency can be a challenge when working with over 200 partners on a global scale, so we have installed strong quality checks (including mystery shoppers and quality assurance audits) to ensure our brand and product is presented consistently.

This means a Mango Magic will taste the same in Melbourne as it will in Estonia. This may seem like a challenge but to us this is second nature.

We select franchisees based on the philosophy, 'It's not necessarily about where they've been or what they have done, but where they want to go and their attitude to get there.' We have some partners whose previous retail experience has made their transition into our stores quite smooth, and also many others with no previous experience who have taken it all in their stride and ended up operating very successful stores. The only common stream among the partners is passion for the brand, following the system and understanding the concept.

I have heard a lot of stories about partners who have cried tears of joy at the news they've been approved as a Boost franchisee and, on the other hand, stories of unsuccessful applicants who have phoned to rant and rave (including one person who sent Boost a doctor's invoice because his wife had to be sedated after hearing the news of their fate).

Boost's recruitment process is transparent. On the Retail Zoo website, we've posted answers to about 90 per cent of the questions we're most frequently asked, including how much it costs to become a franchisee. (You can find these and other resources at www.retailzoo.com.au/franchising-information/.) The application is quite an intense process. After filling out a 'Quick Expression of Interest' online, applicants have to fill out an 18-page questionnaire and send it to us with an application fee. We then call them for a chat. That's the start of the process. There are then more stages to pass before approval is granted.

As mentioned, once franchisees are in the system, they take part in a three-week training program. They work in their store with one of our experienced people for support. They have full access to our team and we do our best to ensure they succeed.

Surrounding yourself with greatness

The business grew from strength to strength, and we were able to employ some other key people to help run it. I still proudly take my hat off to our young team in the early days, and I'm amazed at everything we achieved together and the number of daily problems that we solved. The success of the business was a real credit to them. I was in my thirties and my team was in their early twenties: in addition to Jacinta and Kristie, Naomi Webber was an accountant and our savvy CFO.

Kristie had a large care factor and a thirst for knowledge that helped keep us out of trouble. When I first met her, Kristie was a junior lawyer working in the leasing department of a law firm. I would spend hours with Kristie going through the leasing contracts line by line, asking her to explain exactly what every clause meant. After she came to work at Boost, Kristie went from only looking at property leases to needing to know everything related to business law. She was in her element. Through diligent research, she ensured that every decision made was the correct one, creating order and building a strong foundation on which this fast-moving beast of a business could grow. Very early, we had good corporate governance, unusual for such a small business at the size we were. We have made many mistakes in our business, but, largely because of Kristie, fulfilling our legal requirements was one thing we got right. And this was a critical part of the foundation of the business.

Because of an earlier hiring error, Naomi was presented with an absolute mess to fix (which she did). Naomi was a young accountant recommended by Geoff Harris (more on him later) and we hired her as the CFO. The accounts at the time were in a terrible state but, to Naomi's credit, she built up a strong team and after many months of all-nighters she got the accounts back in order. Accounts tend to be that boring area that entrepreneurs think of as unimportant, but not having correct numbers and clarity on what your business is doing means you're running your business in the dark. The numbers tell you exactly where to put your focus, which team members are thriving or struggling, and, more importantly, give you a solid business in which you can trade. Naomi helped give us that clarity.

And Jacinta, a woman with no franchising experience, learned all aspects and helped make the franchising tactic a success. Jacinta had great tenacity in achieving the required goals, no matter what it took. I remember her telling me once, 100 per cent seriously, that she did not understand why people missed deadlines. She rationalised that if your head was going to blow up if you missed the deadline, you would make sure you met it. So, really, no-one could have a reason for missing a deadline. From that time onward, we had a saying that something was a 'head-exploding deadline'. The other saying that got us through those times was 'eat that frog', from the book of the same title. Every day it seemed there were hard calls to make, and no-one likes making hard calls, no matter how tough that person seems. We often referred to those days as 'eat that frog' days.

Seeing Jacinta develop over those years was incredibly rewarding. While at Boost she achieved AFR's *Boss* Young Executive of the Year award as well as the Telstra Australian Young Business Women's Award, both of which she deserved in spades. I have travelled many frequent flyer miles with Jacinta over the years, setting up Boost internationally. From meeting with sheikhs in Dubai to looking for sites in the snow in Estonia, it has been a remarkable journey.

Together, Kristie, Naomi, Jacinta and I worked out the problems as they occurred. All of us were learning and doing things for the first time, but we had an enormous care factor to get it right. It truly was girl power! And in the high-paced growth of Boost, we never would have achieved what we achieved without the strong girl power from these three young, smart, passionate women. We often laugh that a year at Boost was like working five years anywhere else. It was both scary and exhilarating pulling the business together and we had a ball. Many nights were spent with pizzas, working into the early hours of the morning. Sitting at a round table with these women, there was always a feeling that any problem could be solved, and when we all went in our different directions in the business we all knew that no-one was going to drop the ball—we would achieve what needed to be achieved.

Jumping in—and thriving

According to Kristie, everyone being in over their heads was part of Boost's secret: 'We were all in over our heads but that kicked us into survival mode and we performed at our best at all times. It made us appreciate and value one another. There was no place at Boost for negativity, cynicism or doubt. Everyone at Boost's support office embodied the company's mantra—being passionate, healthy and determined to be the number one franchise in the world.

'J's minimum expectation of you was that you knew what you were talking about. You couldn't bluff with J. She was always happy to nut something through with you but only if you understood the problem, openly explored solutions and had a "can do" attitude. Mistakes weren't tolerated—mistakes can let others in your team down—but to not try at all was inexcusable at Boost.'

Everyone in my small initial team played numerous roles. We had to—we didn't have a team of people sorting out the various solutions to problems. We all wore various hats: the accountant, the secretary, the publisher, the negotiator and the cleaner. We did everything behind the scenes. For the first two years, I worked from the kitchen table at home, while my first two employees (a PA and a part-time bookkeeper) used the dining room.

Having the business operations in my home also allowed me to be around for my three boys. I have always been a great believer in the idea that children should be in your life, not you in theirs, and they will have a richer life because of it. That is how I resolve the guilt that comes from being a working mum. But I also had a secret weapon (then and to this day)—my mum, Joan. I honestly could have never achieved the level of success I have without her. People call her 'Saint Joan' for good reason—it's with her help that I manage to maintain a balance between home life and the passion for my businesses.

Almost every day, Mum drove from Boronia to my house in Malvern East, a 60-kilometre round trip, to help me with my children. Not only did she do the drive and dedicate her life to helping me, but she also did this without trying to produce any guilt in me whatsoever. When I told her in a moment of guilt that I was asking too much of her, she told me that she loved every minute of it and it made her life complete.

I remember a day when I was in Sydney and Mum called to ask what time Jeff was getting home to look after the kids. I didn't know, so I told her I would call her back. I eventually got hold of Jeff to discover that he was in Brisbane for two days. (Nothing like great communication between the two of us.) I then called Mum back to let her know about my incompetence—that neither Jeff nor I was within 1000 kilometres of her and I was not going to win mother of the year that year. Mum just laughed and told me the kids would be fine.

Mum also had that ability to not cross from the grandmother role into the mother role. The second I walked in the door, she would defer to me for everything. She is the perfect grandmother and, for me, the perfect mother. She has eleven grandchildren—and four great-grandchildren—and has a special bond with each and every one of them. So much so that at Christmas every single one of them flies from interstate to Melbourne, bringing their current boyfriends and girlfriends with them, for Mum's Christmas lunch. Mum didn't know what she got when I was born. Even now, she openly wonders where I came from. But she has been the most amazing support for me, and I love her from the bottom of my heart.

If my mum is the perfect grandmother, my father is the perfect grandfather. I take my hat off to him for being able to sit for hours and hours playing games with his grandchildren, letting them paint and even plait his hair. He has a great attitude to life; he is 87 and still umpires cricket and plays golf twice a week.

The business would also not be the success it is without Jeff—he has been with the business every step of the way. I lean heavily on him for advice and guidance. Particularly in the first couple of years, I was terrible at firing or counselling people, so I used to go to him for anything that was confronting. His greatest attribute was his absolute confidence in what we were doing and in my ability to pull it off. When I walked in the door completely stressed, he would calm me and tell me everything would be fine. This was largely because he was such a 'big picture' guy he had no idea of the day-to-day problems or cash flow. His full-time job allowed him to only keep his thumb on the macro picture, and sometimes stepping back and looking at this bigger picture was exactly what I needed. Twenty-five years on, he is still my best friend. Together we make a wonderful team, in business and in life. Jeff unlocked many things in me that helped create Boost.

Running at full tilt

At the end of 2001, we had survived our first year of trade. We had four Boost stores, including one in Melbourne's Jam Factory (a popular shopping and entertainment complex). Boost had reached the point where the business was truly taking over the house. I was using the kitchen and dining room as offices, our master bedroom was the CFO's office, and Jeff and I were sleeping with the boys in their rooms. Jeff used to complain that the only action he got was me doing the laptop dance, as I typed until all hours of the night. I remember walking past the dining room one day, looking in the room and realising I'd reached the point where I hated not getting away from the business. I was working 17 hours a day. For my sanity and for my family, I decided Boost would have its own proper home. Up-and-coming young businesses need a great deal of cash, so moving from my home to an office was a huge step financially, but it was also a big decision emotionally. While the move meant my boys would no longer be running under my legs while I was talking to suppliers or working out a solution for a customer, I had really enjoyed still being so close to them—and there is nothing like a child's hug any time of the day.

In 2002, we thought it would be a good idea to join forces with our competitor, Viva Juice. They had four stores and we had four stores. At the time, I was feeling things were getting over my head. The business was taking over my life and I needed some of the work taken off my hands.

We met with the owner of Viva and discussed a deal. Perhaps not surprisingly, they wanted more than what we thought was reasonable; in hindsight, though, not being able to merge the two businesses was the best thing that could have happened and it was a real turning point for me. I realised I had no-one else to turn to—the net didn't exist. It was up to me to nail this business. Jeff was great with securing new sites and helping me develop the marketing plan, but the nuts and bolts were all on my plate and we had everything on the line. I loved what I was doing and the adrenaline that came with running a new business. I was not always 100 per cent confident in what I was doing—okay, that's an understatement.

I was not even 50 per cent confident in what I was doing—but the reality was I was the biggest expert out there in this specific area. I had no-one else to approach and I just had to work it out along the way. (More to come on the Viva story later.)

It was also around this time that the media really started to get interested in the Boost story. Basically, it felt like I was two people—I had *Janine*, the founder of Boost Juice, and *me*, the person who was employed to get PR for Boost Juice. I had to see 'Janine' as a tool to use to get people to understand what Boost Juice was about. Through my experience at UIP, I had sat through dozens of hours of interviews, and one thing I learned was that you have to be yourself—you cannot fake it. So that is what I did; I was just me, in all the interviews. I was always honest and transparent, and told the truth about Boost's journey and any mistakes along the way. What made talking about Boost easy was that I was (and, of course, still am!) genuinely so passionate about the company and the brand, so it was my favourite topic to talk about.

I was just me, in all the interviews. I was always honest and transparent, and told the truth about Boost's journey and any mistakes along the way. What made talking about Boost easy was that I was (and, of course, still am!) genuinely so passionate about the company and the brand.

As time went by, and with each problem solved along the way, I perhaps inevitably started to feel more confident in the decisions I was making. During those early years, I made sure that I understood every aspect of every decision I made. To me, the fact I cared so much about the business justified my behaviour. I painstakingly took the time in every area to come to the right decision, from dealing with the franchising and trademarks to working on supplier relations. I was obsessed with the business. We rarely used outside companies for areas such as franchising, legal (where possible), marketing or advertising, because I wanted to make sure everyone who worked on something for Boost had 100 per cent focus on Boost at all times. I was a total control freak, needing to know everything. I found it hard to trust that the job would be done well by other people. The reality at the time was no-one on the team, including myself, had been in the business long enough to know exactly what to do all the time.

Back then, it would stress me to my core if I went on holidays because I thought the business would fall apart. Clearly it did not; we had great people doing great things.

Creating brand 'Janine'

In 2002, Boost was flying and the team was obsessed with its objectives; we didn't have all the answers, but we had a great board of wise-heads to help keep it all on track strategically. According to Jeff, Janine moved out of the 'scared little rabbit in the spotlight' position and took the lead with gusto. Jeff says, 'The company demanded a true leader, and it got it with Janine. Along with her band of three young, female executives (who all fed off each other), she achieved the impossible.'

Around this time, competing against 44 other start-up juice bars, it became apparent Boost needed an edge. According to Jeff, 'Most of the other juice start-ups were set up by business guys who put someone in to run it, or other male entrepreneurs having a crack. Janine was unique, and having just read Anita Roddick's *The Body Shop Book*, our simple question was, "who was Australia's leading female entrepreneur?" Poppy King — the 'lipstick Queen' — came to mind, but she had just fallen off the business perch. No-one else sprang to mind, and certainly no-one with three kids and a needy husband. I bounced the theory around with Janine, she readily agreed and we decided to make use of her PR background. The story of the woman with the three young kids who saw a need in the Australian market for a healthy alternative became a reality — and, wow, did it take off. We were in the hottest category. Janine was perfect media fodder: likeable, funny and beautiful, and she showed that a woman could do anything. She was an inspiration to the woman who wanted it all.

'So, reiterating — the company was flying. Her team was amazing and now the media was all over her with very positive stories. She could have seriously become unbearable. In truth, this was the massive confidence boost she needed to build self-belief. Not a fake facade of confidence, but a true core belief that she was good at her craft — which was building a company. Of course, at home it occasionally spilled into a bit of tension, with both of us being self-important. We had to rework the relationship model and as we did, right before my eyes, I saw an amazing transition in Janine's personality.'

5

STRUCTURE FOR GROWTH

The most important gift you can give to your business in the early stages is to get great systems and strong financial information in place to manage all the mission critical aspects of your operations. The number of people who tell me they have everything in their head is frightening. You cannot grow unless you create a solid foundation. Very early in the Boost journey, we discovered the value of systems—particularly when we decided to move to a franchise model. Strong systems will save you when the going gets tough because—like military training—they give you something to fall back on when your brain is in a fog and you have a thousand urgent things screaming for your attention at once. I was fortunate that my brain works in systems, and every day I was either tweaking or creating a system so the business could grow. Of course, no system will work unless you have an A-team in place to ensure that, as the business grows, it develops into a relatively sleek and streamlined operation. Without good systems and a winning team, you risk creating a scary 'Frankenmonster' of a business that will need a lot of pruning and restructuring down the track to get it back into shape.

It's also important to consider what the future shape of your business will be and make sure the important decisions you make in the early days take you closer to that goal and not further away from it. In the case of Boost, franchising was on the cards from the outset, but franchising isn't right for every business so consider carefully what the best model will be for you. Another thing that set Boost apart was our marketing, which I talk more about in this chapter.

Spend some time in the beginning to think through what your business will need and set yourself up for success early. Remember—you cannot build a house on cracked foundations; you need to make these foundations as robust as possible. The hours you spend early on will save you weeks, months or even years of pain—and potentially substantial sums of money—in the long run. Learn to love the 'boring stuff' as much as the creative side of your business.

Mixing up your marketing

It is no accident that Boost Juice achieved 94 per cent brand awareness in juice and smoothie drinkers in Australia in just five years. After all, having a terrific product is pointless if nobody has ever heard of it!

Much has been made of Boost's marketing and, the truth is, it should be. We weren't the first juice bar, but we were the first in most people's minds. At one point, there were 47 different juice bar brands vying to be in the top two to survive. Boost was the brand that made it through.

It may be old school but the philosophies of Ries and Trout, covered in their book *The 22 Immutable Laws of Marketing*, were followed to a T. This is marketing defined simply as 'find out what customers want and give it to them'—but it's only half the story. The other half of the story for Boost was finding things that customers could *talk* about and giving them to them. So consumer desire and innovation became our mantra.

Early on, so that we had a flag for our team to point to, we came up with the 'Boost JAM Factor', which still stands today. *JAM* stands for Juxtapose, Assimilate and Make your mark, as follows:

- *Juxtapose:* If the other guys do it, we don't! What can we do because we are small and don't answer to a marketing committee? Things like the 'What's ya name?' game (where customers receive a free smoothie if we call their name), or 'Boost Vibe Challenges' (where customers do crazy stuff for free smoothies). Another promotion that was a huge success for us was the 'Give away a Boost store' promotion. We ran this in conjunction with a major radio station, and it formed the station's major rating promotion for the year. The concept was a bit like *MasterChef*—we short-listed 100 people and then worked with these contestants and, eventually, through a series of workshops and interviews, reduced the list to 10 people. We then reduced the list even further, until we got to a final three, all of whom were given a key—and the person with the key that opened the door to the store owned it. (We were worried that the winner may end up not being satisfied with the win—after all, not everyone is suited to being a business owner; it's hard work and not everyone understands the reality of running your own business. So we had a fallback—in six months, the person could choose to keep the store or take $50 000.) The exposure from the promotion was incredible—sales in the state in which the promotion was held went up 20 per cent and we received over $1 million in free advertising. These are all things that the big guns of the world couldn't do, and they're innovative and new food retail ideas.

- *Assimilate:* Find ideas everywhere and from anyone at any time. Tweak these ideas, twist them and blend them into another 'by Boost' idea. Never stop searching and assimilating ideas from the Boosties (staff who work in the stores).

- *Make your mark:* If you do something, do it big! Don't be included in the 'and thanks to…' list with eight other sponsors. Do one big thing great, for maximum cut through. Using this basic formula, we smashed into the minds of Australian youth, and they loved it. These Australians are now in their thirties and forties and still drinking Boost.

Why our marketing strategy worked

Here are some of the reasons our marketing strategy worked (in no particular order):

- *Belief:* As Simon Sinek says, 'people don't buy what you do; they buy why you do it. And what you do simply proves what you believe'.

- *Vision:* 'Love Life' was our soul. If something could make people smile, we had licence to do it.

- *Loyalty:* Our Boosties believed in us and were proud to work in our stores. Because of this loyalty, ideas were well executed in store.

- *Saying yes:* We told staff to not think too much about an idea, just have a crack, and say yes! Some of our ideas may not have become a reality if we had put them to a vote.

- *Radio:* We couldn't afford television advertising, but radio was incredible for building our brand. We still only buy breakfast spots on high rotation.

- *Pillars:* We know what supports our brand: taste, the experience, health and me. If even one of our pillars gets a crack in it, we put energy and focus on it and fix it.

- *Brainstorming:* We allow for the energy flow of an idea, and let even the craziest idea have its space to grow and develop into something magical. When one of the team suggested doing a kids' cup promo with The Wiggles six years ago, it was so 'off brand' for our hip little Boost brand that I had to try very hard not to blurt out, 'No, stop!' The team member worked on it, came up with a vision of how it could all work in harmony, and bingo — we nervously proceeded into one of the best things we still do today.

It's important to push the boundaries philosophically. It's my objective that Boost will have a huge impact on the health of our society—a society that's becoming increasingly overweight. Research indicates that the increase in obesity in children in Australia is in line with the growth in fast-food outlets. I think I'm in a very exciting position to make a difference in the future. If I can create a trend in health and make Boost a phenomenally successful healthy product, perhaps others will see that there's money in health, and they will make more healthy products. I think it's already happening. By promoting our 'Love Life' idea, we're driving home not only brand extension, but also life expansion!

Delegation

Do the words 'control freak' mean anything to you? Okay, I was a huge control freak; I needed to be across everything and needed to know everything — and that is okay if you are running a small team and business. However, if you want to grow a business, you have to learn to hire great people and delegate. Geoff Harris told me once that very few people can take a business from inception to a multimillion-dollar business, and I can see why. You need to change how you think and work as your business grows, as it will have different needs from you — and if you cannot change, you will not be able to be that person who can manage a large business.

For a leader, a lack of delegation shows bad management skills; you cannot grow without trusting people to be able to do a great job, and if you hire well they will be able to do the job better than you.

When Boost first started, I did everything myself. I had to — there was no-one else to do it. There are still days, I admit, when I think, *It would be quicker if I did this myself*. However, I know that I simply don't have the time to do everything. Who does? If I tried to do everything, I'd succeed at nothing.

Of course, I have high expectations of those to whom I delegate. I never choose someone simply because I feel I should, or because that someone thinks they deserve a chance. I always try to hand a task to a person who I believe will do a better job than I could do myself.

I also keep a close eye on how people respond to being given responsibility. Do they deliver? Do they keep me informed? Is the project completed on time? It's all about their actions, not their words. I don't want to be told someone can do it — I just want them to do it!

If you find that you're not getting the desired results when you delegate a task, find another person to do the job. Don't feel bad and don't play along to save someone's feelings. Never reward mediocrity.

Have good systems in place to ensure you, and those you delegate to, stay on track. Much to the horror of all the people who reported to me at the time (and I had 16 direct reports), when things were really ramping up at Boost I discovered the Task icon in Outlook. For those people who are like I used to be (and don't know it even exists), how the Task function works is that you click on the icon and you add in the instructions to the person to whom you're delegating your task. You can add in reports, emails — anything really. You then add the date for the task to be completed by and the person receives a copy of the delegated task. The person doing the delegating also keeps a copy of the task. I even colour-code tasks based on the people they're delegated to ... but perhaps that's the OCD in me.

The Task function was my lifesaver — prior to discovering it, I would have so many balls in the air that deadlines were often missed, there was often confusion on which tasks had been delegated and to whom, and the not-so-great employees benefitted from the lack of follow-up. I started to use the Task system for all my meetings. The rules were simple: I would send you a task with a date by which it had to be completed; you had 24 hours to come back to me if the task was not achievable; if I heard nothing, I would expect the task to be completed. I met with all my reports weekly and we always started with the task list first.

Great people loved the system because it kept everyone on track and on the same page; average people hated it because there was nowhere to hide. If someone missed a deadline, it was there in black and white (actually, in red, because the task goes red when you miss a deadline).

It was not uncommon for me to have hundreds of tasks active. With everything involved with opening over 70 stores in one year, it was critical that everyone kept on track and knew what everyone else was doing. Okay, my obsession with the Tasks function was the standard joke at Boost, and there was even a Christmas skit on my tasking, but it kept me sane and, more importantly, on track.

The key to good delegation is clear communication, with everyone understanding who is ultimately responsible. Setting deadlines is also critical. But when you delegate a task, let the person run with it. Being a control freak, I'm sure that I was probably a bit overbearing in the early days because I wanted everything to be just so, which was not necessarily the best way to go. If you hire the right people in the first place, you can empower them to do the job.

The key to good delegation is clear communication, with everyone understanding who is ultimately responsible. Setting deadlines is also critical. But when you delegate a task, let the person run with it.

Meetings

OMG! Not another meeting. How many times have you had this reaction to a meeting request? Meetings can be powerhouses of ideas and actions, and are great in some ways, because you can get together face to face and you have a great chance to get everyone on the same page. Especially now that our world is so focused on electronic devices, you can find yourself doing much of your job without talking to anyone. But everyone has experienced people misunderstanding the written word, so meeting face to face can reduce these misunderstandings.

But you can overdo meetings and they can be a huge waste of time if done incorrectly. Sometimes, they can just be a group of people sitting around a table putting off decision-making. The difference between good and bad meetings comes down to tactics and disciplines.

Always ask yourself if you really need to have a meeting. Once you've established that a meeting will indeed be the fastest and clearest way to communicate with staff, follow these guidelines:

- Set a start and finish time, and keep the process efficient. Allocating time prevents those rambling, open-ended discussions that are time wasters.

- Set an agenda. This will help keep the meeting on track and on time. Those attending should be given the opportunity to list their own points for discussion.

- Brainstorm and write up ideas or key points. Flip charts or whiteboards are invaluable for getting everyone involved. Remember: there is never a bad idea. Encourage input from all attendees.

- Write down clear actions to be achieved, and next to each point write the name of the person chosen to take care of that task, along with a deadline. By the end of the meeting there should be a consensus of what needs to be done. Minutes must be taken at the meeting, and should be typed up and distributed as quickly as possible. Refer to these minutes at the next meeting to ensure all action points have been completed.

- Send each person the list of action points as a gentle reminder (or not so gentle if the gentle approach does not work) to complete the tasks before the next meeting or approaching deadline.

- Get to the point. Respect other people's time if you are giving a presentation; make it slick and make it short.

- Take it offline. If a discussion is between only two members of the meeting group, the two can meet on that issue after the meeting; do not waste everyone's time on issues that do not concern them.

I remember meeting with someone who was selling me something. I cannot for the life of me remember what he was selling, but I do remember he came into the meeting without an agenda but with a 40-slide PowerPoint presentation. He handed me a copy of the presentation and off he went—each slide was like a novel and he was just reading off the slides. I had to stop him. I then flipped to the last page of the presentation and got the point.

The meeting would have taken almost two hours if I'd just sat there politely; however, at the end of the day, time has to be seen as money. He was a lovely young man, but he did not follow the rules of a meeting. When you're presenting you have to be respectful of people's time. He also thought he was prepared, but it was in all the wrong areas. And he shouldn't have handed me a copy of the presentation. (Never do this—people stop listening to you and start reading.) You need to be clear in meetings and ensure they go for no longer than 45 minutes.

Assumptions

Are your feelings getting in the way of the facts? You've probably heard that to assume makes an ASS out of U and ME. Believe it. When you make assumptions, you let emotions colour your view of a situation. Emotions can blind the smartest people. Some of the assumptions you make about others might be wrong.

Check yourself: are you an emotional person? Do you react to situations, or do you respond? If you react, don't!

A reaction is explosive. There have been times when I've been told a story by one person and reacted by ringing another to blast that person. Then, when the second person's side of the story is put forward, I'm left feeling foolish. No doubt you also have to admit that at some point in your life you've jumped to an assumption and, in your mind, have built a situation up to something it is not. And then you discovered that what you'd assumed was not actually quite right.

I had an executive who used to tell me various things that people were saying or doing in the business. As I trusted this colleague at the time, I would often get angry and act on this information—to then find that I had been told a half-truth. People don't necessarily mean to lie; they may only give you their version of events—a filtered view. When you're handed the objective facts of a situation, or told both sides of the story, a knee-jerk reaction is often out of place. A response is more measured. In this case, you wait until both sides of the story are in front of you before choosing how to reply. I learned quickly that you should always wait until you have the whole story before you act. Acting on wrong or twisted information is a fast way to ruin that great reputation that you have worked hard to develop.

There's no doubt about which of these actions is more professional. Be a person who responds, rather than reacts. Learn to sleep on situations. Keep that angry email in a draft folder for a little while before you hit send. You must also ask questions. It comes back to my philosophy that no question is silly. Asking questions means that you are not making assumptions. It also means that you will have all the information you need to make (hopefully) the correct decision.

Here's how to stop yourself jumping to assumptions:

- Think before you speak. Yes, the story you're hearing may seem outrageous, but you may not be hearing the whole story.

- Try not to make assumptions of any sort—whether you're assuming that someone else will fill the empty printer tray or that a staff member knows what you're thinking.

- Try to keep your negative emotions out of the office, particularly if you are the leader. As the boss, my emotions set the daily tone for the entire office, so it's vital that I keep positive.

- Treat everyone with respect, and respect will be returned.

Respect

Respect is much harder to earn than dollars and it can be more valuable. Respect cannot be bought, sold or traded. You must earn it. In my opinion, having the respect of peers and staff members is the most valuable goal to which a manager can aspire. Your employees don't necessarily have to like you; however, if they respect you, they will listen, understand and cooperate. They will trust in you. If your staff believe what you say, they will follow your instructions. If your customers believe in your product or service, they will buy it.

Showing respect for others is equally important, and the more you do so the more others will give you respect in return. Being an attentive listener is the first way to do this. Never interrupt or mock people when they have found the courage to speak. They believe in what they are saying and you owe them the space to air their thoughts. Try to learn something from them or something about them. By encouraging people's opinions and ideas, by sharing in their successes and not blaming other people when failure occurs, you will earn their respect. Also, if you value other people's time, they will acknowledge that your time is important too.

Respect is much harder to earn than dollars and it can be more valuable. Respect cannot be bought, sold or traded. You must earn it. In my opinion, having the respect of peers and staff members is the most valuable goal to which a manager can aspire.

Always put yourself in the place of the people you're dealing with, and treat them as you wish to be treated. If you give them the respect you believe you deserve, you will find that others begin to treat you in the same manner.

This is particularly important with creditors and debtors. Pay on time and keep the wheels of commerce rolling! You want to be paid quickly, don't you?

Let me give you an example. We'd worked with a particular supplier from the very start—the relationship was great, we liked the company and its staff went above and beyond to ensure we always had supply. This was until the owners sold the company. After this, the relationship started to sour—the new owners were inflexible and did not return calls. The relationship got to the point that we needed to cancel the contract simply to guarantee supply. A meeting was called and a very tall man came in. My hope was that we could either resolve our problems or part company with respect. His strategy was to threaten and use heavy-handed tactics.

From the moment he sat down, there was no respect in the room shown by him for me, which in turn ensured that none was shown for him. It inevitably ended with the only winners being the lawyers. The shame of the whole episode was that if both parties had worked together with respect and with a firm commitment to resolve the problems, it would have ended in a win–win.

If all negotiations are based on respect, even if you think that you got a raw deal, you know that in the future it will all work out. I would much rather be respected than liked. Great leaders are respected. If you are always looking to be liked first, you will find that respect will eventually dwindle.

Here are the components for building respect:

- If people respect you, they will believe in you. This is the cornerstone of good leadership.

- Respect is a two-way street. Treat people with respect and they will respond in kind.

- Attentive listening is an important part of showing someone respect. If you are distracted, people can quickly pick up on that fact and it will make them feel unimportant to you.

Confrontation

Most of us will go a long way to avoid a confrontation (yes—I'm talking to you!) and I used to be exactly the same. Now, however, I've learned to deal with unpleasant situations. I face up to difficult problems at the beginning of each day and get them out of the way.

You won't earn respect for being inactive and pussyfooting around an issue because you don't want to clash with someone. I used to hand some of the more difficult situations at Boost to Jeff (who thrives on confrontation). Now, I see that confronting these issues can be an amazing and cleansing experience. The key is choosing the right way to fight.

A calm manner gives you the upper hand in any argument—if you show control of yourself, you will be in control of the situation. Keep your voice level, your eyes directed at the person and speak clearly and concisely. It's very difficult for your opponent to speak or act aggressively towards you in the face of such composure.

Make sure that you have all the facts you need at your fingertips. I will only get into a confrontation if I have right on my side. If that means I need time to prepare, I will avoid having the discussion until I am ready.

And remember, confrontation does not have to be an argument but rather can be a discussion about different points of view—and it can have a positive outcome! Bully tactics may win a particular battle, but they will lose the respect of all those witnessing or involved in the discussion. There are two sides to every argument. Try to understand the other point of view because, believe it or not, you could be the one in the wrong.

Avoiding 'grey'

As Janine says, in the early years, she sometimes turned to Jeff in times of confrontation because he was simply better at it. Jeff says, 'Well, we are all different and if you're keen to grow in business you have to adapt to your strengths and find points where you can cut through and stand out. I guess a strength of mine has always been to tackle issues head-on—an approach probably exacerbated by the number one mission I was given when I first arrived in Melbourne radio: "Go in and kick a few doors down." This mission was given to me by the radio's senior management, who were frustrated at the amount of "grey" they were seeing. ('Grey' includes ineffectualness and wishy-washy actions and leadership, as well as the inability to make a firm call on anything. Grey allows people to say that they were confused and uncertain about what was required. It is a weak person who lives in grey.)

'There really is so much grey in the world and it often seems much more practical to confront a person on an issue and get it sorted then and there. In practice, of course, it very rarely works out that well in the short term, because you catch the person on the hop and they go into massive defensive mode. Very little may get resolved at this point—but don't be fooled into thinking nothing has happened. The confrontation usually has a massive aftershock.

'I once had to confront an executive over a pretty serious matter. During the meeting he was amazingly calm and collected, even ambivalent over some of the issues I was confronting him with. So much so I was almost questioning my facts. However, I then tracked his movements after the meeting—and he went into overdrive, with eight phone calls and six emails on the subject within an hour. So, yes, the point about what needed to be sorted did get across.

'The other great thing about confrontation is that it's often only under pressure that you find out the type of person you are truly dealing or working with. How different people respond to confrontation can be a real eye-opener. Obviously, the best types of people take it on the chin, work out solutions and move on.

'While I'm all for tackling something head-on, if you are going to confront a person, remembering all of Janine's rules in this area is critical. You must be in a position of power with regard to your knowledge of the facts. The initial electric volt that starts the confrontation will give the person a shock but you need to be able to follow up with facts to show you know your detail.

'Confrontation should be seen as cleansing for everyone—it shouldn't be a shouting match but should (hopefully) be a calm (and sometimes awkward) delivery of something that needs to be addressed. Once you've addressed the issue, you can all move on.

'The reason appropriate confrontation is so effective is because so many people avoid it—so issues are allowed to grow and fester through your business. Good confrontation stops or at least diverts the stream of bad practices you are trying to prevent. So start to think about the things and people you need to confront. Obviously, bringing up issues is much easier if you're in a position of power, but the truth is if you confront issues for the improvement of the business with people above you on the chain, you'll likely be looked on with admiration for the courage that you've shown.

'Confrontation is certainly not for everyone, but if you can learn to enjoy it and use it effectively, you will certainly stand out from the pack. And remember—the quicker you tackle something head-on, the better.'

Here's how to deal with confrontation:

- Aim to ignite and extinguish an issue in one meeting. Have the confrontation face to face, and keep coming back to the facts to support your point of view.

- Always attack the problem, not the person. If you can avoid injuring egos during the exchange, the relationship will always recover much more quickly.

- Don't take it personally. I've always found this difficult, as I am a passionate person, but I've learned to follow this advice. You cannot respond in a calm and intelligent manner if you take things to heart.

Here's how to take your confrontation skills up a notch:

- Take notes during your business dealings. If a confrontation brews, you can avoid a 'he said–she said' mudslinging match by showing supporting evidence that backs your position. Remember—you cannot have enough written support.

- Avoid email fights because they can be misread—and they could come back to bite you later.

Money

William Shakespeare knew what he was talking about when he said 'Loan oft loses both itself and friend', and nothing much has changed in 400 years. It's always easier to lend money to a friend than it is to get it back. Don't do it! Learn to say no.

If you're running your own business, also learn to say no to any unnecessary consumption in the short term. For the first three years of running Boost, I didn't take anything out of the business, not even a salary, and I put everything I could back into the business. During those years, we lived in a rental property with three kids and the business. Everything was on a budget.

When you start a business, suddenly you have lots of friends who want freebies. Start how you intend to finish. Even to this day, I pay for my smoothies and juices and, if I shout someone, I pay for it. In a cash business, you can be tempted to take money or give a mate a free drink, so the easiest way to stop this is to act in the way you want everyone to act. You may feel like a tight arse for not giving your friends free stuff, but all these 'freebies' cost money—you pay for them. Do not feel guilty about charging for products and services. Keep your friends, family and business as separate as you can.

The other thing to note on money is that it is all that matters. In other words, you can have a great profit but the only thing that matters is what is in the bank. Even when buying a business you only care about the amount of cash you put in and the amount of cash you take out at the end of the day. If the amount of cash you take out is a lot more than what you put in, then it is a success. That is business in two sentences. No fancy names, no tricky accounting: it is all about cash.

Here are some things to keep in mind about money:

- Cash is king. No matter what else you think about and focus on, without cash you have no business.

- If you build a reputation for never lending money, it will be easier to say no to requests. When I invest I make it clear, like Geoff Harris did when he started with me, that I am not a bank. The business needs to run as a business and together we need to solve the money problems of the business.

- Offer your time and advice to those seeking help; those forms of assistance are much more valuable than cash in the long term.

- If running your own business, try to forgo short-term gratification for the long-term success of your business. Ask yourself whether certain personal purchases really need to be made or whether the money would be better invested in the business. Every cent spent should return double. Ask yourself: is this expenditure really necessary right now and will it return me profit?

Negotiation

A negotiation is not successful unless both sides feel they've won. In line with this, two elements are vital to a successful negotiation:

- *Information:* Do not go into a negotiation with only your point of view. Understanding the other party's needs is equally as important as understanding your own. Ask yourself, 'What do I feel is reasonable?' or 'What would I want if I were them?' This will allow you to counter the opposition's arguments before they are raised.

- *Lack of emotion:* The only way to negotiate a great deal is having the ability to walk away. The only way to know if it's a great deal is to listen, listen and listen. Never let your heart rule your head in negotiations. If you are emotionally attached to something, you will give away too much. This holds true whether you're buying a house or making a business deal. Try not to take the proceedings personally. It's difficult, but try to think of yourself as a third party.

Negotiations take an enormous amount of courage and a very clear head. You should always ask for more than you want and then negotiate down. Don't give away your minimum requirements—you may end up with even less. Also, don't favour the same weapon over and over; it will become less effective each time you use it. The more options you have, the more power and control you have.

I remember my first major negotiation—we took on a small juice chain in Queensland that had started up with the name Juice Boost. In the end, we paid for them to change their name and we bought their trademark. It was a win–win situation. We had to pay, but it was worth it to retain the purity of our brand. We had right on our side and got the best out of the deal!

I have negotiated all sorts of things—including bills from lawyers who in my opinion have overcharged me (perhaps not surprisingly, this happens a lot), multimillion-dollar master franchise agreements and sales of businesses—and the biggest thing I have found is that no negotiation is the same. The greatest skills you need in any negotiation, however, are emotional intelligence and the ability to be a really (really) good listener. If you listen more than you talk, you will hear what the other party wants. The other great skill in negotiation is putting yourself in the chair of the person you are doing business with. (Remember—the best negotiation is when everyone wins. If you cannot put yourself in the other person's shoes, you should not be negotiating.)

In 2005 I was in Dubai with Jacinta, negotiating a master franchise agreement with a party we thought would be a great company to open Boost stores in Dubai. We wined and dined with their sheikhs, we listened to their needs and we presented our business with the passion and enthusiasm that we have for the brand. The business spoke for itself—it was a sexy brand, and was in the wellness category from a country that is perceived to 'love life'. They had the contacts and experience to launch the business in the market and were ready to move into the wellness category. We negotiated the contract while we were there, constantly working on the memorandum of understanding in our hotel room. I remember being with Jacinta in the airport on the way home when it was all over, not quite believing that we had completed an amazing deal to launch Boost in Dubai with a party who had never seen a store.

Here are the core elements of great negotiation:

- Learn as much as you can about the other party. If you're negotiating with a public company, you'll find that everything you need to know is easily available—from information on the shareholders and senior executives to the company's profit forecasts. Information is your key weapon.

- Try to stay detached during the negotiation. Emotion has no place when you're making a deal.

- Put yourself in the opposition's shoes. This will help you to counter their arguments and provide a win–win solution.

- Know what you are prepared to accept, but never give away your minimum. Aim high and negotiate down—never the other way around.

Success

There is a price to be paid for success. No-one achieves their goals and dreams without sacrifice. But can you afford not to try?

What have I given up? A hell of a lot of time—time with my family, husband and friends and also time on myself! Is it worth it? For me, yes. That's because the results are not just financial success—I also love the journey of creating something special, as well as the mental stimulation and the chance to follow creative pursuits. My success has made me a better, more rounded person, and I wouldn't have given up what I did if I didn't want to. Sometimes when I'm torn between work and family, I feel like I'm robbing Peter to pay Paul, but it comes down to what's worthwhile for you. My whole life has been a pendulum, trying to get the balance right, but that is what makes life interesting.

If you want to follow your dreams, you need to be prepared to make sacrifices; you must decide what you're willing to put in. Many people expect luck to deliver them a fortune—well, I've got news for them and it's all bad! Success does not just come about magically—you have to make it happen, and that means giving it everything you've got. With any luck, your hard work will pay off. It has for me and I have no regrets. I have a great life and nothing to complain about. Can you ask for more than that?

Of course, success means different things to different people. My sister Lisa is 21 months older than me, and I remember being in the car with her when she was 17 years old. She said then that what she wanted in life was to find love, get married and have a family.

Lisa has never not gotten a job she went for, and at every job she gets they love her. However, even now her family is her success—I look at her three girls and her husband, whom she loves, and I really see success. Happiness is success, not dollars. I am sure that Lisa has never looked at me and my business success and wanted my life, because she is already happy and successful. I am successful because I have a husband I adore, and kids who are all individual and amazing—because that is what makes me happy and that is my success.

Here are some things to remember when chasing success:

- Be prepared to give your all to achieve your dreams.

- Success is not just monetary (or sometimes not even). Do what you love, and the financial rewards will come.

- There are no fairytales—there is just damned hard work!

Communication

Most conflicts and problems start with a lack of good communication. Great leaders are always good communicators. Never underestimate how important it is to have a 'catch-up' with people, and to communicate effectively and consistently. These days it comes in many forms: social media, email, Zoom, face to face...the list goes on. Each platform has its own positives and negatives, but nothing beats a face-to-face conversation. One of the things I learned on *Survivor* is that face-to-face conversations and interpersonal skills are really good for relationships and, frankly, good for the soul. There was nothing like sitting in front of a fire (while very hungry) with nothing to do but talk. There were no smart phones buzzing, no-one was fixated on posting on Instagram, everyone was present—which enabled relationships to grow and flourish. It made me realise how bad I was off the island and how much time we all spend with our noses facing our smart phone screen. More importantly, how much we are not focusing on our loved ones around us. How often do you see people at restaurants having a romantic dinner while both are on their phones? We all need to make a change. We are all so highly stimulated and obsessed with our phones, no wonder stress and poor mental health are so common.

Everyone talks about good communication...but how do you go about it? When we think about 'communicating', most people tend to have talking in mind. However, communication comes in many forms, including verbal, social media, email and other written communication (remember that thing we used to do?). Given that we spend so much time emailing and texting, it can be overwhelming when you're faced with the prospect of speaking to a group of people. You don't have an opportunity to 'backspace' or 'delete' if you blush, stutter or stumble through a speech. My good friends will tell you that I make words up. They are nearly the right word (cringe) but there might be a letter missing or I simply change the letter. I sometimes am going so fast that my words get messed up. This unfortunately has been the case my whole life, so I just laugh at my own stupidity and move on. If you ever see me give a talk, listen out for the odd crazy word.

Good presentation skills offer you the opportunity to leave a positive and lasting impression on others. You don't want to be remembered for the number of times you flicked your hair or adjusted your tie. If you are, your message is hopelessly lost. Make no mistake—the audience will judge you on your performance.

Do you need some work in this area? Not sure? Try taking a video of yourself in action. Is that the image you want to project or are you cringing at your performance the whole way through? (Don't worry if you're a bit embarrassed by the sound of your own voice at first—most of us are.)

Confidence is the key to a good presentation and you can gain the poise you need by practising and refining your skills. Plenty of courses in public speaking are available. They cover all the essentials—dealing with nerves, projecting your voice, cultivating the right image through your appearance, delivering your key message and the secret of the 'pause'—as well as other skills you can nurture and adopt.

Most tutors will advise that your natural style should not be changed completely. The best course of action is to refine and improve your inherent ability. If you attempt to adopt a totally foreign persona, you will come across as insincere. This is an important aspect I have learned about communication and developing your communication style—be true to yourself. It's fine to take tips from other people, but still do it in your way.

I have been asked to tell the Boost story a number of times and, in the early days, I could never quite do the story justice—the way I told it just wasn't quite right and I knew I wasn't communicating the ideas clearly enough. Then I saw a presentation by Simon Hammond, who had put us in his top 20 list of wonderful brands. He is one of the few people we have come across who truly understands the power of the brand.

We heard he did a great presentation on brands so we asked him to present at our annual conference. His presentation was *wow!* It was a show, complete with music and interesting snippets from the internet on marketing ideas. He made us laugh and almost cry with the emotion of his presentation. I was so impressed that I asked him afterwards if he could help me formulate my story into a great presentation. We spent weeks (and weeks) pulling it together and getting to the truth of the story, and also the true essence of what I am naturally like as a presenter.

We found my presentation could vary greatly from day to day, depending on the audience. In essence, I was a confident player if I felt like I had engaged with the audience—if they laughed and nodded, my presentation was pretty good (if I do say so myself). But if I didn't feel like I had connected with the audience, it was normally a disaster. Simon assisted me with understanding who I am and what my natural style is, with the added help of a few videos and props to ensure my communication is consistent. The main point has always stayed with me—whatever you do, be you.

Regarding email, be sure to investigate correct etiquette and read your emails thoroughly before clicking the 'Send' button. (Be wary of 'Reply all'!) Be courteous and remember that the ramifications of an email can be with you a long time; email can be subpoenaed in a court of law! If I have an important email that I need to send, I write it, then send it to myself to read later as the reader would, and then I re-edit it.

On the subject of phone calls, don't do anything else while talking to someone on the telephone—it degrades the conversation. The sound of your fingers typing on a keyboard is a sure sign to the person on the other end of the line that you place little importance on the person and the conversation.

Here's how to polish your communication skills:

- A professional speaking or presentation course is an investment in your business future.
- Be professional in all your business communications, be they typed or spoken.
- Learn to use technology to your advantage.
- Give all your attention to the person to whom you're speaking, whether it's face to face or on the phone.

- Treat email communication with care. It may be an instant medium, but the message can come back to haunt you.

- Poor communication is the number one reason for conflict.

Customers

Many businesses talk about being customer led, and mostly it is simply hot air. When businesses goals are motivated just for the money, then good luck on being successful. A great business has to always have the customer in mind, first, second and third. If they can accomplish this the money will come, but not without their customer.

As Boost has grown, I've found that I've gotten further away from the 'on the ground' customer experience. As the manager of a growing company, you ultimately move on to the next level of development in your business, delegating tasks to others. You become more removed from the day-to-day running of the company—and you can miss the simplest problems. Try not to make this mistake and never be a stranger to the frontline. Don't ignore the very hand that feeds you. Always, always make the time to speak to the people who are facing the customer.

I work hard to counter any movement away from the frontline. It's vital to continue to tap into the root of your business, and for me that means going into a random Boost store and queuing up with the other customers. Or when I'm in the office I might answer a ringing phone—any phone. If it's a customer wanting to vent frustrations or even give positive feedback, I talk to that person one on one. I ask questions about the company and the level of service received; I ask for people's opinions. It's a simple task, but an extremely valuable exercise because it allows me to derail potential problems that may be quietly simmering away.

One tool we use to encourage feedback is our Boost Juice Guarantee. Every store displays this guarantee, and you can also find it on our website. If you do not have a good experience, let us know and we'll fix the problem. And we absolutely do fix it, every time. What's more, we offer customers a number of easy ways to get in touch with us, and we employ several staff members to take care of customers and respond to customer feedback, including one full-time staff member, a weekend support person and two social media coordinators.

Resolving customer complaints immediately and effectively is critical; our policy at Boost is to respond within 24 hours. Customers are usually so grateful (and surprised) to receive a response, their problems are easily resolved. This is a vital and mostly unseen part of our marketing strategy.

Whole books are dedicated to the subject of creating and keeping loyal customers, so the main thing I am going to stress is this: love your customers; *truly* love them. And if you are the leader of your company, make sure that every day you find out what your customers are thinking and wanting; this knowledge will flow through to influence all your behaviour.

Treat each customer as if your business depends on them. Because it does.

Get angry when your customers aren't treated well, and fix every customer problem with vigour—they are your life support system. Hire frontline staff who like people. Every Boost store has a multitude of talented people, specifically chosen for the role they need to play in the customer's experience. We've even given each role names. 'Eva', who is bright and bubbly, is on the front counter greeting the customer. 'Ian', introverted but super-diligent and process-oriented, is making the smoothies. And finally 'Beth', a real extrovert, is on the last station—pour up. This person is the last impression customers get of the brand, so (hopefully) she hands over the finished product with a big smile. We don't always get this process right, but it is indoctrinated into our belief and it is what we strive for.

Make the love of your customer an absolute pillar of your company's beliefs and you're on the way to success.

Here's how to focus on your customers:

- No matter what your position in a company, never take your customer base for granted. Keep in touch with your market and respond quickly to its needs.

- Small problems can become large if not dealt with quickly. Put systems in place to ensure customers never feel ignored.

- Customer liaison is vital and should be part of your marketing strategy. Word of mouth is your best friend—and can be your worst enemy if you don't address issues.

Putting the systems in place

Is your business ready to grow? Have you got the systems in place to support your operation if you experienced sudden, unexpected growth? Ask yourself the following:

- Do you know what kind of business structure you're trying to grow?

- Do you have a mid- and long-term business plan?

- Have you developed good systems to support day-to-day operations?

- Have you developed good systems to support your future growth plan?

- Is your team fully trained and supportive of your business systems?

- Does your business stand out from the pack? If not, what are you doing about it?

- Are you developing the characteristics that will give your business the edge?

6

SCALING UP FOR THE WIN

Any new business is hungry for cash, and Boost was no different. In 2002, we needed more money to grow and we had two choices: get other investors into the business or find the money ourselves. We decided that we didn't want to sell down by taking on additional investors, because it would be like working for someone again and that was the last thing we wanted. However, this didn't change the fact that we needed cash and fast. We decided to jump off that entrepreneurial cliff—and then went from strength to strength (with one or two major speedbumps).

In 2002, the banks wouldn't touch us with a 10-foot pole because our only asset was our family home (which the bank already owned most of), so we had to find money some other way. My greatest fear was losing the house that Jeff and I had worked so hard for. (Admittedly, Jeff worked really hard to buy our house. While I was gallivanting around the world, Jeff was saving money. He purchased his first house as a 19-year-old—who does that? He was saving for a house and I was sailing around the world with David Bowie. The 'Gods of Yin and Yang' must have had a good laugh when they put us together. But he had assets and I had debt—a perfect match in my opinion.)

In the end, we risked it all. We sold our only asset, the family home, and invested all the money into the business. We packed up the kids and moved the family and the business into a rental for two years.

Picking the right mentor

By the end of 2002, we had opened 15 stores and were going strong. There were 50 stores opened by the end of 2003. I could see a permanent frown on my brow — it seemed to have cut deeper into my forehead every morning. I was learning as quickly as I could. I did not have mentors; in fact, I did not have friends. I did not have time to sit down for a coffee let alone a chat. One morning in 2002, I was sitting at my desk when I saw a note to call Geoff Harris.

I had spent most of my adult life abroad so I certainly was not up with the 'who's who' in business (and these were still the early days of Google), but it turned out this Geoff person wanted to meet and discuss the business. Geoff wasn't the first person to show interest in the business, and we were very guarded about who we wanted to 'play' with. We did not know much, but we did know that we wanted great people around us to enjoy the journey with. We had already rejected many, many offers from people to get involved.

However, Jeff and I decided I should meet with Geoff Harris at a café. We sat down and he showed me the latest *BRW* Rich List. (*BRW* was the Australian business bible.) Upon reading his name and his worth in the Rich List, I spilt my entire coffee onto his lap and note pad. Not the best start to a relationship. Now, you may be thinking, *What a show-off*, but he simply wanted to show us that he was not a tyre-kicker. Geoff was someone genuinely interested in us and our business. I quickly learned what I probably should have known already — he was the co-founder of Flight Centre, one of Australia's great success stories. And, for the record, you could not find a more generous, kind, loyal and considerate man on the planet.

Recognising a winner brand and a cultural fit

In 2002 Geoff Harris was starting to wind down his day-to-day duties at Flight Centre and was looking for a young brand where he could assist the owners in growing their business. After reviewing a number of brands in 2001, he came across the Boost Juice store in Melbourne's Doncaster Westfield. According to Geoff, 'I quickly recognised that the brand was a potential winner in the "healthy to go" sector just as people were starting to realise how unhealthy the traditional burger and chicken "to go" outlets could be.

'I phoned Janine and talked about how she was going and the challenges she was facing with a young family and a fast-growth business. Janine and I met at a local coffee shop to further discuss the business to see if we were "culturally" compatible and our business goals were aligned. It was a great meeting and it was clear that culturally it was a fit. Janine was so enthusiastic about her brand and business that, in a gesture of enthusiasm, she spilt the entire contents of her coffee all over my newly acquired leather diary. The stains and the stuck-together pages were a constant reminder of that meeting and of Boost. After that meeting we agreed to meet again, this time with Jeff. After meeting both of them, I was excited about the prospect of becoming involved with this retail start-up.

'There was no question in my mind that Janine was a "young gun" on the go with plenty of energy and a great concept, and total honesty. She just needed some rounding at the edges and a sounding board for her growth as she ramped up the business across Australia (and later overseas).

'The other key element in my deciding to invest was that Jeff Allis was part of the deal — and that was vital, because his marketing and ideas 'grunt', combined with his radio background, added a unique element to the partnership, as did his backup and support for Janine.'

Over the next four months, Geoff gave us 'precious gems' of strategic business foresight and never asked for anything in return. By the fifth month, we were ready for him to get involved.

Some months prior to this decision, I had stopped doing the accounts and hired a CFO. I quickly discovered this recruitment decision was a mistake and I learned the first lesson in hiring the right people. The CFO I hired was previously employed by a business that had gone belly up. I'd assumed this would have given her hard-learned knowledge on what not to do; I was wrong. The figures we presented to Geoff Harris to review seemed to be all wrong. When his accountant said not to move forward, because there were problems with the integrity of the figures, I was alerted to our CFO problem. It wasn't that she wasn't trying; it was just that the job was too big for her.

Geoff did eventually buy into the business and we hired the right person to get the accounts balanced. I was thrilled to have him become a part of Boost. Geoff's buying into the business was simple; we agreed on a price, he handed me a cheque and that was it. I know lawyers are a necessary evil but if business deals could be done based on a handshake and someone's word, profit margins would certainly be a lot higher.

The handshake deal

After a short review of the numbers and many meetings later, Janine and Geoff agreed that he would invest in the company and he acquired 24 per cent equity in Boost holdings. A handshake deal cemented the relationship and, according to Geoff, 'this formulated a level of trust that was vital in the early, stressful days of growth. Both I and Janine were co-directors, and we wore the risk of offering personal guarantees, and took on the pressure from the banks and financiers/landlords/staff and so on. But, as the saying goes, without risk there is no reward. We both powered ahead with complete trust in one another.'

In the coming years, we worked closely together and the direction of Boost changed in many positive ways. I spent many, many hours on the road with Geoff, looking at stores and picking his brains. We would meet at least once a month, and during these meetings I would always bring out my long list of questions about various issues that I was having at the time. Geoff is one of the good guys; he is honest, loyal and a true Aussie bloke if ever there was one. Geoff expanded my personal business knowledge dramatically.

Adding a Boost to Viva

As Boost was growing, we were always on the lookout for growth and synergies, so we had a relationship with our competitor Viva Juice. As mentioned, in 2002 we had a chat about merging but, due to unrealistic valuations, nothing eventuated. Two years on, however, we ended up concluding a deal for the purchase of the Viva Juice business. By that stage, we had over 80 stores and they had 24 stores, all owned by Viva and not franchised. They were the only real competitor we saw in the marketplace, and the owner had secured some great sites in the Melbourne and Sydney airports, which prevented us from getting into these positions.

The acquisition was a monumental learning process on all levels, because it was the first business that I had ever bought, so off I went on another massive learning curve—this time, learning all about acquiring a business. I learned the difference between a share sale and an asset sale, for example, because if we got this wrong it could cost us thousands in tax and risk exposure. Getting solid advice and working with consultants and lawyers that we trusted was critical. The legal arrangements were extraordinary, and the process was painfully long and detailed—in all, the negotiations lasted six months. In some respects, however, the process was aligned with my strength of being detail-oriented. And even though it was stressful, it was invigorating to complete.

My girl power team (Kristie, Naomi and Jacinta) came into their element through the Viva Juice acquisition. As I mentioned, in the beginning none of us really knew what to do—we were all doing it for the first time. However, we all cared enough to make sure that we got it right, which we did. The research and pulling of favours from all of our contacts ensured that we made the acquisition a success. Kristie was beside me until the final sign-off on the deal. I have now watched Kristie go from being a keen and passionate young lawyer to being a married woman with two beautiful children and her own law consulting firm, and I am so proud of what she has become.

Turning the tables on the 'experts'

According to Janine's early lawyer Kristie, Janine's is the kind of intelligence that's 'always refreshing to be around because it's the "raw kind" that stems from a curious mind'.

At meetings with Janine, Kristie says, 'I enjoyed watching her level the playing field. If we met with someone with expertise in a chosen area, often the meeting would start with the "expert" (lawyer or otherwise) lecturing Janine on what this person assumed Janine did not know. The expert's assumption was often right and Janine would openly admit it, which would make this person act even bolder or sometimes more arrogant. of course, that's when Janine would "turn the tables". She may not have known what the expert was talking about at first but, by asking a few simple questions, she would very quickly understand the topic. And then with one swift statement she would turn the tables and leave the "expert" dumbfounded.'

On the very last day of the Viva deal, I was called into the legal office in Melbourne's CBD to finalise a number of minor points, having been told this would only take 30 minutes at most. I had been having dinner with some friends, so I remember arriving at 8 pm. The Viva owners were in the other room going through the so-called minor points. Issues started to go back and forth between the rooms, so we decided to get into one room to finalise these points. We left the boardroom at 11 am the next day. In utter disbelief, I clearly remember watching the sun come up; we had been negotiating all through the night. I do remember a couple of emotional outbursts and one walk-out, but the deal got done. Strategically, this was a great win for us; mentally it was *OMG!* We were already growing at a store a week, and now we'd thrown in converting an additional 24 stores and getting the Viva staff on board—it was a great lesson in change management. I remember hearing the Viva owners cracking champagne and celebrating the sale; all I could think about was what I had to do next to make this work.

Tired messes after the all-nighter, Kristie and I found a local gym where we could have a shower. Jeff met me at a café in the city and, I admit it, I had a bit of a meltdown to my husband that day, and may have demanded that he buy me something that 'blinged'. After four years of growing the business and realising what was on my horizon with the additional stores to bring on board, I was beyond tired and emotional. I must have had a furious look, because Jeff went straight into a local jewellery store and indeed bought me something that 'blinged'. The funny thing is, I am not even into jewellery; but it helped to signify another chapter in the journey.

Business Woman of the Year

As I've mentioned, franchising worked for Boost. At the start of 2004, we went out for dinner to celebrate our successes. The business was now turning over $1 million a week. And 2004 continued to be a massive year for us, with the Boost machine of training, building and marketing in overdrive. We were opening a store a week, and every day I seemed to be creating another spreadsheet for a system or process. The people who reported to me called me the 'Task Queen'. (I had discovered how to use the Task tab on Outlook by this point, and it was my saviour.) I could now effectively track the millions of moving parts that were Boost.

In 2004, we were also in 'The Top 7 Businesses' in *BRW*'s annual list of top 100 fastest growing businesses in the country. The hysterical thing was that same year I made the list in *BRW*'s Young Rich list. The reason this was so funny? We had not taken a cent out of the business; every dollar made was put back into the business. For the first three years, I didn't take a salary. In year four, I did and it was $35 000. I was one of the lowest paid staff members at the time. I went shopping the day the article came out. When Jeff saw all the bags and raised an eyebrow at me, I smugly said, 'Have you not read *BRW*? Apparently I can afford it!' That day, I wanted to make sure that the next time I made the *BRW* rich list, it would be true.

And this was the same year that I won the Telstra Australian Business Woman of the Year award. I was absolutely thrilled, surprised and honoured, and the award was a pivotal turning point for me. The awards ceremony was the first time in over four years that I had networked. I had sourced out businesspeople here and there for lunch and their advice, but never in a larger group. With this award came the opportunity to meet some of Australia's most amazing and inspirational women. One was Launa Inman, who was the managing director of Target Australia at the time. Her journey from South Africa to becoming one of the leading businesswomen in retail in Australia is profound. I have enormous respect for Launa—not just as a businesswoman, but also as a friend. The other person I connected with was Judith Slocombe, who started out as a vet. She had her own pathology business that was purchased by Gribbles, and she's now the CEO of The Alannah and Madeline Foundation. What she has personally done for this foundation is quite extraordinary.

Both of these women have also won the Telstra Australian Business Woman of the Year award. They too are mothers and wives facing the similar challenge of balancing their lives with their love for business. All of us enjoy what we do. We have a passion for creating and driving forward this think tank we call business. Between the three of us, we have 15 children (Judith has the lion's share with nine). Although we do not catch up as much as we would like, we meet at the national Telstra awards dinner annually and are on the end of the phone whenever needed.

Cracks in the foundation

We were hot! Revenue was pouring in. Store sales were increasing year on year by nearly 30 per cent. Obviously, all the partners were happy and making money. We seemed to be flying. That's when the cracks started appearing.

The first crack was something that I didn't even see coming. The success of the brand meant franchise opportunities were in hot demand—and our early franchise partners knew it. They were on-selling their businesses, sometimes for five times more than they paid for them. We could not legally then (and nor can we today) tell people how much they could sell their businesses for. However, problems emerged because the banks were lending to the incoming Boost franchisees, helping them to cover the premium sales prices. The consequent enormous repayments were making it difficult for the new franchise partners to make a profit.

I sourced out Lesley Gillespie, one of the founders of Bakers Delight (a company that had also used franchising to expand), and she told me this was a common problem. I was a massive fan of Bakers Delight and still think they are another true Australian success story. Lesley is a down-to-earth, no-nonsense woman who right from our first meeting was warm and likeable. Bakers Delight had been around for 25 years at the time, so they had gone through many of the same issues we were now facing. She shared some of the solutions that worked for them, such as the system they used for franchisees to report their financials (she was kind enough to actually give me the spreadsheet as well as permission to use it), and how they trained their incoming franchisees.

A number of uncontrollable environmental factors also put enormous strain on the 'new' franchisees, in addition to some of the large loans. The second crack in our success started when *A Current Affair* (*ACA*) ran a story on juice bars, attempting to show they weren't such a healthy option (which made my blood boil, because we do everything to be healthy). Remember—Boost isn't just about selling smoothies and juices. It's about offering a whole experience that ends with, 'I feel good about myself for choosing Boost'. For example, you walk into a store, the music is playing, there are bright, fun colours, and happy people and delicious fruit are all around you. Ideally, you're served by a smiling, happy, young person, and you walk away with a great experience and a healthy, great-tasting product. Now, if we get any of these things wrong, the concept will not work.

Boost isn't just about selling smoothies and juices. It's about offering a whole experience that ends with, 'I feel good about myself for choosing Boost'.

ACA stated that juice bars were adding sugar to their juices, and that one juice or smoothie was equal to a Coke or a Big Mac. Our first reaction was that no-one in their right mind would believe the story—that we physically added sugar to our juices or that having a soft drink or a burger was equivalent health-wise to a highly nutritious juice. To our surprise, some people actually did believe it. To add to the drama, *Today Tonight*, the main competitor to *ACA*, did a story paralleling the claims about juice bars. This really got the public questioning whether Boost added sugar to our juices and smoothies, and wondering if our products were indeed as healthy as we said. I was horrified. I could not believe that people had started to doubt us. I thought if they saw how rigorously we vetted every product—if they realised how much time and effort went into taste, health and delivery—they would never believe these claims.

And then, as if this predicament wasn't bad enough, the Australian Competition and Consumer Commission (ACCC) got involved. With over 50 competitor juice bars opening their doors, some claiming all sorts of health benefits, the ACCC stated that they would be investigating all juice bars and their claims. The problem was this: Boost was the largest juice chain, so people just assumed we were the 'juice bars' the ACCC were after. The ACCC investigation was never directed at us, because we complied with all requirements and rules; our health claims on each product are 100 per cent backed up and documented. The customers did not know this, however; they only read the headlines.

The icing on the cake (if you will) was when Bondi Council in Sydney blamed Boost for the litter on the beaches in their area. I found myself on radio station after radio station defending our honour against the ACCC and Bondi Council. Over and over, I explained that we had never and would never put sugar in our juices—and surely people were responsible for putting their own rubbish in the bin.

All of this attacked our core principle of 'I feel good about myself for choosing Boost'. Sales went from exceeding forecast, to flat, and then to negative growth. When your business starts to go in the wrong direction, it takes everything you have to stop the slide and turn it around. The worst thing: people believed what was written about us. It was simply wrong and unjust. I was crushed. What I needed to do was 'get over it', start to look within the business for solutions and not be a victim.

During this insane time for Boost, Jeff was amazing to have on my side. Having been in the tough, ruthless world of radio for 22 years, he had learned a thing or three and enjoys a good battle. (I think Jeff has read every war book ever published.) He is a very strategic thinker and sees the 'big picture' quickly.

The first thing we did was hire a lawyer for advice. We believed what the networks did was misleading. We contacted both networks and worked out an agreement, and they then assisted us in getting the correct message out in the media.

The second battle was the perception of our packaging and, by extension, its environmental cost. Were the cups we used the best product for the environment? We contracted an environmental firm to compare and contrast. At the end of this report (and a dozen other reports we checked), it was conclusive at that time that foam was indeed the best product for takeaway packaging. (Of course, new developments in packaging are always taking place and so we review our products on a yearly basis. Based on these reviews, we have now moved to a paper product for our cups, and we will continue to look at ways of creating a lighter footprint on this planet.)

The third thing we did was hire a well-known nutritionist and hop on the PR train to get our message out: 'A smoothie or juice is always a healthy option!' Our philosophy on health is really simple; in fact, Dr John Tickell explains it the best. He says people would not have a weight or health problem if they did not worry about the latest diet fad, but instead followed the low-HI diet, or low-human-intervention diet. In other words, a diet that includes food that is as 'close' to the tree or ground as possible, and contains little or no processed foods. Let's not kid ourselves—if you read the back of a packet, can or bottle and find a ridiculous amount of numbers and words that you cannot pronounce in the ingredients list, you know that's not low-HI food.

By implementing these strategies, we were on the road to fixing some of the root causes of the external cracks at Boost, not just bandaging them. I could finally breathe.

Checking our internal cracks

All of the solutions mentioned in the previous section were great and they worked, but our biggest success came through picking up a mirror and looking hard into it, to see where the really major problems were. We had gotten complacent, arrogant and reactive. Growing to over 100 stores in four years meant we had also started to show some cracks internally, including in our staff training and systems. Our stores were looking tired, and so was our team. We just were not attacking every part of the business—so that's exactly what we did.

Geoff Harris's view was that we needed to keep the business compartmentalised, which would then make people accountable for their own areas and expenses, and reward people for their successes. So that's what we did. We broke each part of Boost into simple pieces. We began to get back on our toes and think proactively, reviewing and changing how we reported, cutting $2 million in expenses, and building a strong profit-centred mentality in the business. No longer was there a black pit of expenses, as we reviewed small things, such as printing double-sided and only in black and white, as well as larger areas. We renegotiated everything we could, from our auditing and accounting costs to our raw ingredient contracts. We worked harder and smarter. The business became better because we took a hard look at ourselves—rather than blaming the world for our woes.

Our largest market was New South Wales and the whole state was going through a recession at the time. We knew that if we could turn NSW back into positive growth then the rest of Australia should follow. Part of the marketing campaign to get back on track was hiring the latest hot hunk, Tom Williams, as our brand ambassador. Jeff also came up with the 'Week Day Sucks' campaign, which was cheeky and on brand. Where companies were saving costs by cutting marketing, we did the reverse and invested heavily in PR and marketing, running tactical promotions on television, press and radio.

On the HR side, I again spoke to Lesley (from Bakers Delight). She was generous not only with her time but also with her tools, which never in my wildest dreams had I expected. During our meeting, we discussed all sorts of topics, including the challenges that she had faced growing a franchise network. Most of our discussion came back to the same thing: people. The horror stories were people-based and so were the success stories.

Systems and processes are the heart of a franchise network, and from my meeting with Lesley I realised Bakers Delight were light years ahead of us in their systems and knowledge. Lesley was more than happy to give us any system that would help and also allowed our executives to meet with her executives to see what each department could learn from the other. (In fairness, we were doing more of the learning than they were.) Many of the systems that we use today are a result of those meetings with Lesley.

After meeting with Lesley, we reviewed our training regime and HR strategy. These improvements at Boost were so effective they reduced our overhead by nearly $1 million.

We then looked at the stores that were looking tired, and started to upgrade both our company and franchise stores. This investment worked tenfold—each store that was upgraded immediately had an increase in sales.

From these few, meaningful process improvements came a dozen more; from this dozen came a dozen more, and so on. This was the tipping point and it spread throughout Boost like wildflowers.

This was a pivotal time in the business. The positive outcome and lessons learned made Boost the strong business it is today. Once we were back on the road to success, looking back and remembering all the stress and uncertainty that this period brought made me realise the downturn actually made us a stronger, more systematic and a substantially better company. When people ask me what our worst time was, my answer is, 'You have to have hard, challenging times to be great.' Going through the fear that your business is in trouble is no fun at all; however, what makes a business great is what people do in the turbulent waters, not what they do when it is smooth sailing.

When people ask me what our worst time was, my answer is, 'You have to have hard, challenging times to be great.'

The experience also taught us a great deal about ourselves. Jeff was the 'it will be okay' person, while I was the 'problem solver', running on fear and adrenaline. I knew the risks of everything we did and all the 'what ifs'. Jeff was big picture, and did not share my fear of failure. His attitude and calmness (probably based on not knowing the details!) kept me sane.

The stress that you go through when running a fast-growing business is enormous; Jeff had that ability when I walked in the door to make me feel everything would be all right. Without Jeff's calm energy, I would have fallen into a heap during this time. I know I mention Jeff a lot through this book, but that's because he has had the biggest influence on me. (So if there's a little repetition, it's because he deserves it.) Jeff has helped shape the woman I am today. He had more faith in me than I had in myself, and for that I am eternally grateful.

Most of the executives on the Boost journey have also made a huge difference. I've already mentioned just some of the many people who were a part of the initial team. I cannot say this enough: if we had hired the wrong people at the start it would have been very difficult, if not impossible, to get Boost to where it is today. Mark, our former CFO, created the financial systems and processes we have now, enabling us to truly grow. There are also many franchisees along the journey whose passion and brutal honesty helped us to continually improve.

Hitting the wall

After the domestic improvements, the international side of the business had also picked up significantly and my focus was to grow that side of the business (I felt like it was my new 'baby'). The intricacies of contracts and the differences in the countries and cultures suited my background. We were dealing with people from all walks of life, in places I had never dreamed I would visit. From Arabia, with men in their long white robes, to Estonia, where we had to walk in the middle of the road so we were not killed by falling snow from the rooftops.

I was obsessed with getting the international side of the business up and running, but this kept me away from my family for over three months a year. My work–life balance pendulum was angling all the way to the work side. I had started to develop into a strong, confident businessperson (well I thought so anyway) with significant knowledge on how to start a business and make it a success, and had formed very strong bonds with people in my team; however, I was losing touch with my husband and family.

Going at this ridiculous pace, it was inevitable that I would get to a point when there was nothing left in the tank. Trips to a health retreat every year had helped, but there comes a time in every business that the reins need to be shared. This brings new ideas, experience and passion to the table. I believe it is vital for a business to have fresh ideas and enthusiasm to continually grow. In 2006, I met with Geoff and Jeff for coffee and we started to look at a succession plan; two years later, I was still holding the reins and the business was still growing at a massive pace. We wanted the best person and we were prepared to wait for them.

Balancing the scales

At 40, Jeff decided to step down from his role as group program director of Australia's biggest radio group, Austereo. Boost was going from strength to strength and, according to Jeff, 'financially we were okay, but at this stage not through Boost, because we still had not taken any money out of the business'. Jeff had signed a three-year consultancy/golden handshake deal, so he decided it was time to have a year off and take stock. The 'taking stock' process highlighted a few shocks. Jeff says, 'How bizarre — I decide to relax, take a year off, and it almost costs me my marriage.

'All of a sudden, the scales were tipped: Janine was in high-powered, global-expansion mode and I was in total unwind mode. Her self-importance, her three months of travel overseas a year, her long hours, her lack of consideration for family time, and her 20 texts each hour (bantering about work while we were playing with the kids in the park) — annoyed the shit out of me! Truth is, she wasn't that bad. However, taking a step back from my perspective, it was her self-obsessed world of focusing only on Boost — making everything else second — that made me question if this was the woman I wanted to be married to.

'Thankfully, when the crunch came (and it was a big "bang"), we both acknowledged our shortcomings and promised to work on the issues — and we never looked back.

'Almost immediately, Janine made significant changes in her work–life balance. Clearly not working wasn't working for me, so I went full-time into the business as the CEO, while she concentrated on building our global push. At the time, Janine started to realise there was more to life than Boost; it had absolutely taken everything out of her and she had given it everything. She started getting her life back beyond Boost. Outside of Boost she had no friends, no hobbies and no other passions. That's when she had her epiphany.'

On a business trip to South Korea everything changed. I arrived a day early to get rid of jet lag and decided to have a massage. It was an over-the-top, great massage. I even had mud gloves on my hands to get rid of toxins. To this day, it is the best massage I have ever had. I can still see myself lying there. And it was during this massage that I had the most amazing epiphany (although I don't think it was due to the mud gloves). I am not sure I have ever experienced such a strong, absolute feeling, and I still find it difficult to explain. In that moment, I just knew I wanted to have another baby. There was absolutely no logical reason for having this feeling. Was it because I knew my biological time was up? Was it the toll of too many days spent entrenched in a 'man's world'? At the time, I was a director in the Hawthorn Football Club, an Australian Rules club, and in this and my other business groups I was one of very few women. Perhaps what I felt was an unbelievable desire to nurture, or simply it was a great excuse to step away from the business for a little while.

I was so excited after the massage I could hardly contain myself. I had to speak with my husband and tell him. I knew I faced a few problems before I even started. First, it would be impossible to reach Jeff because he was doing some work in Fiji. Second, per my request seven years ago, Jeff had had a vasectomy. So I did what any modern woman would do in the electronic age—I emailed him. I simply wrote, 'I want another baby'. My husband is a man of very few words and within an hour I had a reply: 'Sure!' I don't know what was going through his head at the time. He was probably laughing at me, because the vasectomy must have crossed his mind, but 'sure' was enough for me. My goal was to have a baby; now I just had to solve all the problems that were stopping me achieving this goal.

Five minutes after getting the 'sure', I did a Google search on vasectomy reversal. I came across a microsurgeon who was based in Sydney and who just happened to be the surgeon who did the first hand transplant. He was also part of the team who performed the first face transplant. South Korea was approximately on the same time as Australia so, after a few wrong attempts, I got to speak to the doctor. He said there was normally a six-month wait but he'd had a cancellation on Wednesday and could do the surgery that day. 'That's fantastic—book him in', came flying out of my mouth. Far away, my unknowing husband was sunning himself in the beauty of Fiji. He was completely unaware of the plans I was putting in place. Of course, he had said 'sure'.

I arrived back to Australia on the same day Jeff arrived back from Fiji. Timing is everything with Jeff. I made sure I was prepared and waited for the right moment, which came after we had put our three boys to bed. We were relaxing with candles and wine. I had the lighting at just the right level. Jeff casually referred to my email. 'Oh that', was my attempt to downplay my hours of frantic research and phone calls. Suddenly I couldn't hold it in and blurted out all the facts and data; the romance went out like the candles. I was speaking so fast, but Jeff just sat back, smiled and said he would do it. He suggested that we start the research on reversing the vasectomy. My eyes widened, 'No need—I have found a surgeon who is world-renowned.' Jeff didn't say anything, so I pressed on. 'We are *sooooo* lucky because he can do the surgery this Wednesday.' This took Jeff back a bit and, after a long pause, he said, 'That would be my birthday!' Needless to say, I did not win wife of the year—although I did spend more on his birthday present that year than I had in all the years we had been together.

Jeff's vasectomy reversal was a success in theory; however, three and a half months and many failed tests later, none of the sperm were alive. We also interviewed for international adoption. Almost a year from the date of my epiphany, we were still no closer to having another child.

This baby continued to 'tap' me on the shoulder from wherever she was, telling me to make it happen. Back to research my options. The next path was IVF and, although this road is complicated and emotional, I felt for me it was relatively painless. However, the first four attempts failed. All this was happening while Boost was growing leaps and bounds. We began to look into domestic adoption when a friend suggested a doctor in the United States who'd had amazing success. Because we were always travelling for Boost, we thought, *Why not?* After a further few unsuccessful attempts—finally, we were having another baby! I was 42 years old and going to be a mother for the fourth time; I could not have been happier. Jeff had been so supportive of me and this decision, from his first 'sure'. Watching him with his daughter and witnessing the love he has for his 'princess' makes all the effort of all those years totally worth it.

Even with my focus on bringing the very much wanted Tahlia into the world, there was no question that we still had to grow—all businesses do. But growing any business and developing a brand is extremely difficult. Having successful systems and processes in place makes it easier, but people still tend to underestimate how hard it is to actually grow.

While Boost still had significant growth potential, we also understood it was not about growing Boost anywhere we could put a store; we were very strict on where we believed the Boost brand could be successful. At the same time, international growth was amazing, with 12 countries signing a master franchise agreement. Signing agreements to open Boost stores overseas is one thing; however, opening stores in these countries was slower than expected. Then it hit us—we were just so focused on growing the Boost brand domestically and internationally, we were not exploring other options.

Building a Zoo

We have always believed in the value of holding strategic, working retreats with the team, to evaluate where we have been and where we need to go. It was during one of these off-site retreats that we asked a single, simple question: 'What are we good at?' A few hours of brainstorming and numerous whiteboard scribbles later, we discovered what we were good at wasn't our fluffy bits of marketing; it was our boring back-end. We were *great* at business, franchising, IT, design and development, legals and finance. These were our cornerstones. These back-end departments gave the business the strong infrastructure required to grow. My annoying focus on every detail and refusal to outsource these departments were the keys to building these cornerstones into the foundations of our business. At the end of this exercise, it all seemed obvious; we'd identified what we were good at and would utilise that to grow.

The advantages of Boost's 'profit culture'

The cultural wiring of Boost was a 'support centre' that was team-based and focused on providing a 'fee for service' — in other words, people in every department thought of themselves as their own little business. According to Geoff, 'A "profit culture" was reinforced strongly throughout the group. From each department's members to all the company and franchise shop teams, a non-hierarchical structure was vital for the company's growth. We also introduced reward and recognition nights, and annual conferences and award nights to recognise key achievers, and welcome new franchisees and new ideas into the Boost family.'

After much discussion our strategy was to create a new parent company — Retail Zoo — of which Boost would be the foundation brand. Retail Zoo would facilitate the growth of strong, small businesses, using our proven back-end and marketing skills to make these concepts successful. The brands we would look at growing had to be pre-existing and had to show evidence of being successful models. Often the entrepreneurs who started these kinds of concepts struggled to take their businesses to the next level. Largely, this was due to lack of expertise and the resources required to do so. Retail Zoo, however, had both the financial and intellectual resources to take a four- to 10-store business model and grow it within Australia and around the world. What you discover when you speak to businesses of all sizes is that strategy is 10 per cent of the success — execution is where the real value lies. We had the know-how to execute a concept into a successful brand and business.

Once this strategic step was made, everything fell into place. To be honest, after me growing Boost to where it was at this stage, the business needed new legs to continue the journey. Jeff was fresh after a year's break and we were ready to swap roles; he was chomping at the bit to make his mark on the company. Jeff became the CEO, Retail Zoo was born and we started the journey of buying up-and-coming brands.

Strategy is 10 per cent of the success — execution is where the real value lies.

Jeff came across a brand in Chadstone Shopping Centre (in Melbourne) called Salsa's Fresh Mex Grill. I've always been a fan of authentic Mexican food and the variety of dishes it offers — while I don't like Mexican food that's stodgy, heavy, dull and uninspired, I love Mexican food that's made with fresh ingredients such as coriander, red and green chillies, tomatoes and limes. We have our own Aussie version once a week, and it's such a great way for the family to put together their favourite combination.

Like the smoothie and juice industry when we started Boost Juice, when we first looked at Salsa's Fresh Mex Grill there was not really a 'fresh Mex' category in Australia, or not one that was well known. In the United States, Chipotle Mexican Grill was growing a market in this fresh Mex category, after early investment from McDonald's. Salsa's Fresh Mex Grill had four company-owned stores and they were operated by Lawrence Di Tomasso—a wonderful man with a real passion for his food. The financial numbers coming out of the stores were amazing, thus proving Lawrence had found a successful fresh Mex formula for the Australian palate. We invested in the company and then, a year later, purchased the whole company. Since then, we have taken Salsa's from four stores to over 50 stores (at the time of writing). The Mexican wave is here, with a number of contenders now in the marketplace—again, a very similar trend to that of the juice market in 2004. Like the juice market, the fresh Mex market will settle down to a couple of dominant players. Lawrence is no longer in the business; he was handsomely rewarded and is now building his next concept.

Salsa's was an excellent addition into the Retail Zoo family. Like any business there are challenges and Salsa's has had its fair share. All businesses have their cycles and you have to prepare for the ups and downs. I foolishly did not realise when I started that business was not linear (hello!). Business has certainly taught me differently, that you have to fight every day to have a strong business—there is always a battle to have in business and you have to navigate through each brand's cycles.

Change is one of the hardest things to manage and Retail Zoo was no different. Retail Zoo went through its own transition period, moving from everything being about Boost to a situation where people needed to think, and systems needed to be bigger and broader. Managing this change led to one of Jeff's greatest skills: his ability to hire great people. We have two different leadership styles—I am more hands-on, while Jeff is more hands-off. His looser reins allow his executives to thrive, and his new ideas and approach have proven to be incredibly successful, taking Retail Zoo to the next level.

Under Jeff's leadership he had Scott Meneilly, who was the GM of Boost, and Mark Slattery, who was the CFO. They were a great team, Scott being the creative entrepreneur type and Mark the steady hand for the finances. Business was booming and all the signs were going in the right direction. Jeff was looking after the domestic market and I was driving the business forward internationally; the business was strong and the team was equally as strong, but it is not always that way and there were many more lessons to learn.

7

LEAPING INTO NEW MARKETS

Travelling for Boost took me back to those early years wandering the world before Boost began — and between missed flights, lost luggage and stumbling straight into meetings without sleep, it sometimes felt like I hadn't advanced much on my backpacker days! Definitely those early years as a traveller helped to prepare me for the rigours and surprises of working in new environments overseas.

A rainbow of culture

Focusing on international markets and travelling for Boost meant I experienced all kinds of amazing cultural practices, from the boardroom to national festivals. I have honoured the practice of Ramadan during a visit to Malaysia and sat opposite a full Arab board, in traditional white flowing dishdasha, in Kuwait. On the king's birthday in Thailand I have worn traditional yellow in celebration, and acknowledged the hierarchy order when entering a room. I've even learned the simple but important ways to present your business card in different cultures.

My most memorable day-to-day experiences come from sampling local fruits as we localise the menu in each region. Each location has its own unique local fruits — some of which I'd never tasted before—and this made for some very interesting tastes. Some that were not necessarily that good, but some that were amazing surprise discoveries!

A major challenge of working internationally is the language barrier. This sometimes requires interpreters, extending even to the interpretation of body language. It was interesting to discover that some gestures are not universal—and some gestures you really need to keep to yourself in particular countries if you don't want to offend people in the street! Sometimes simply being a woman in business is novel in itself. In some countries we visit, women have the same rights as men in the workplace. But this isn't the case everywhere and we have experienced countries where the notion of gender equality does not sit easily. Through personal experience, foreign businesswomen will be treated with great respect and courtesy but, regardless of the actual seniority of our party, there is still an assumption that the male present will naturally be the decision-maker. But I have never found this to be an obstacle for me in business—again, there is a lot to be said for the power of being underestimated!

Rise of a global empire

Back in the early days of Boost, when we were running the business out of our own home and testing recipes in the kitchen, I never thought I'd be writing about how our little operation had grown into a global empire. But having grown Boost into Australia's largest juice bar, focusing on taking the concept offshore seemed a logical next step. We now have over 600 stores operating throughout Australia and around the world, and we're operating in more countries than any other juice bar in the world. This far exceeds my wildest dreams at the start of the journey. We've seen absolutely amazing growth, with an average of two countries and 30 stores opening somewhere in the world each year for the past four years. And the journey isn't over back home either, with new stores opening in Australia every month.

You have to grow your business; it's your job as a business owner. Each year you need to grow the business and find ways to improve and be the best you can be, and growing internationally was one of the strategies that we implemented to achieve this. Our international strategy was not to look at a region and focus on it, which is what many advisors would tell you to do. Ours was a 'master franchise' strategy, where you grant the right to a partner to grow your brand in another country. For this strategy to be successful, rather than focusing on finding the right region, you need to focus on getting the right international partner—a partner who understands the brand and what it takes to be successful. They need the right capital and the right attitude and then maybe they will succeed. Unless you have done it, no-one truly understands how hard it is to create a brand from scratch. It takes time, money and sometimes everything you have to create a brand. It has taken over 10 years to get to a point where we have finally got some critical mass in some territories, but the vision to be the world's most loved and known brand will become a reality—I'm just not sure exactly when!

Pausing to reflect

The birth of Tahlia gave me and Jeff time to reflect on what was important in our lives. After riding this incredible 50-foot wave of business, we asked ourselves, 'What do we really want out of life and what does the future look like?' At the time we were over 14 years into starting Boost and, even after creating Retail Zoo, we had all of our eggs in one basket. We were also aware that we needed more expertise in the international markets—although we were having some success overseas, we knew we could do it better.

Since the beginning of Boost, we have owned various percentages of the business during different times. I had never been overly concerned about the percentage we held. I focused more on the value of that percentage, having enough percentage to ensure that we maintained control of the direction of Boost (which is an important lesson—know thy shareholders agreement). Other than that, having the right partners was always the more important aspect of this balance, and making certain that all partners could contribute within their field of expertise.

Throughout the whole journey of Boost Juice, we had talked about the many ways of growth. Going public into the ASX was discussed a number of times. We spoke to a friend of ours who was an expert in the field and he described the various options. One was private equity (PE). We had never considered PE before as we had heard some horror stories from people who had gone down that path. If you have an open mind, however, you never know where this can lead, and that is what we adopted. We began to research all of our options and realised the right PE partner would provide us with capital out of the business for personal use and put capital into the business for growth, also allowing us to find someone with strong experience in the international marketplace.

We retained the services of a friend's financial services company, Wingate, embarking on a new learning curve—selling part of our business. The important thing for us was that we maintained real control of the business —we would still control the day-to-day operations. Where our chosen PE partner came in would be to assist us in our international expansion, share their expertise at a board level and be a good supportive partner as we continued to grow Retail Zoo.

During the initial interview process, we met PE companies that were true shockers—some of which we wouldn't ever consider doing business with, as it felt like we would be playing with the devil. We were then introduced to Riverside, an American company. After meeting all the partners in Riverside, we were quite comfortable they could meet our objectives and would be a good fit for Retail Zoo.

We started discussing a possible deal with the partners at Riverside. Selling part of my fifth child was an excruciating experience for me. However, I knew it was the right move to make on a very personal level, enabling us to take hold of opportunities that we have always dreamed of.

We still maintained a major share in the business and, more importantly, we still controlled the day-to-day operations of the business. The reality of any decision is that you never know for sure how it will play out. There is always a 'honeymoon period', when everyone is on their best behaviour. Fortunately, it turned out that our new investors are good to work with. The honeymoon period was over and Riverside continued focusing on what they do best—finding new acquisitions for Retail Zoo—and leaving us to do what we do best.

Recognising one of Australia's premier brands

For Geoff Harris, the two key growth elements in the Boost business were first getting to $100 million in turnover, and then to a $10 million profit. Geoff says, 'Both economic indicators proved that Boost had arrived as a very serious business indeed in Australia and was now on the international radar for investors.

'After resigning from the Boost board in 2010 and selling down to a 6 per cent holding in the company to Riverside, I have a real feeling of being part of something special. A brand that is indeed one of Australia's premier brands, and one that has achieved its success with real expertise, class and verve from Janine and Jeff as the founders and main shareholders. They both deserve immense credit for their vision and business skill.'

When PE firms get involved in any business, largely they do not have a passion for that particular business; they simply have a business model. That model is basically to buy businesses for their fund and for that business to return three times the cash back to them in a relatively short period of time—normally between three to five years. Some business founders get angry that they do not understand the business or have the passion for the business. For me it was always clear, as I understand their business model. I do not expect them to get excited about the new juice range that we are launching, or the new digital campaign that has gone crazy. I did, however, expect them to respect how the business was created.

Most people from the PE world have never owned a business and have only been in the corporate arena. They have no understanding of what it takes to grow and develop a brand or how to fix it when it goes pear-shaped. They only have experiences with businesses from the outside. I think sometimes they find the founders, with their passionate drive, a necessary evil instead of the asset that they invested in. I have heard dozens of stories of founders selling their businesses, with the investor happy for them to move on or pushing them out—only to find a few years later that their investment is worth half or less than they originally bought. Business are created with passion and focus. Often it is only the founder that understands the DNA of the business because they created it and know how it ticks. On the other hand, there are some founders who cannot open their eyes to new ideas and get caught up in the past. You have to have a balance of both—that is where the true magic is. If businesses are only just about the money, then the business will be short-lived. Don't get me wrong, thank goodness for PE firms, as they are a great way for shareholders and founders to realise some of the value from their business—and they also know many tricks to drive returns. At the same time, it can be frustrating that they do not understand the business and often make suggestions and calls that are wrong because of this.

Dealing with investors or PE firms is 100 per cent fine if the business is going well. Success gives you freedom and power. Businesses have cycles, and if you are in a more challenging cycle and the business is not delivering the returns then the PE firm can and will jump in to protect their investment. The secret to doing business with a PE firm is be successful.

(I know: easy, right?) They will leave you to get on with the job, release their return and move on to another business.

With Riverside we had enormous success under Jeff's leadership, with double-digit growth. The relationship with Riverside was strong and supportive. However, like all PE firms, there comes the time that they need to move on from the investment and put their shares in the business up for sale. Off we went again, speaking to more PE firms who may want to invest. The process is time-consuming and does take your eye off the ball, but it is also very healthy for a business. I always found that if another business does due diligence on you, they will find all your faults, and I am a huge one on continuous improvement. Often the business is better because of it.

Eventually, with much back and forth, Riverside sold their shares to Bain, a large PE firm once again based in the United States. We really liked the team that Bain had; they were smart and motivated. It was here that we learned another lesson: people leave firms, and those you think you are working with today may not be who you work with in a month's time. With Riverside, we dealt with the same people from the start to the end of the process. Bain had a little bit more of a revolving door, so who we started with was not who we finished with—which made it very difficult for them to truly understand the business. I think my point here is that, when you get into bed with any partner, make sure your eyes are wide open. And always remember why you went down the partnership path in the first place.

How to do yourself out of a job

Jeff and I believe that our job is to always do ourselves out of a job by surrounding ourselves with and developing strong, ambitious executives who are ready to take the mantle and grow. Prior to Bain coming into the business Jeff had made the decision after seven years to step down from CEO and move into the Chairman position. At the time, Scott was flying in his role of GM of Boost Juice: he had converted to paper cups and launched new lines that were enabling the business to really prosper. He had that entrepreneurial flair that is rare in non-founder CEOs. Boost was going strong. When Jeff decided to step down as CEO, his natural successor was Scott. Scott got a new office and a big title and off he went. His leadership style was very inclusive and he was a much-loved CEO who did well for a number of years. Like any business, however, there are cycles, and there are different CEOs for different times in a business. Riverside as a partner were very hands off; Bain, however, were very hands on and deep into the numbers. Being a more entrepreneurial CEO, it was difficult for Scott to have that creative flair; he was torn between the additional pressure of hitting numbers and trying to solve the millions of challenges in each business. It is no mean feat to make sure your business grows every year, and Boost was going okay, but not to the level it needed to be. At the end of the day, it was not a good fit and Scott moved on to other opportunities. While Jeff was very close to Scott and was sad to see him go, we all knew it was time.

Change is always good in a business as it brings new ideas and new enthusiasm…The biggest killer of business is 'We have always done it that way'. I hate that line. I love new people who have a curious mind and can keep changing and evolving.

Scott's departure opened the door for new executives with new ideas. Sometimes a business can get stale with the same people and needs new blood and new ways of doing business. I always love to promote from within, but sometimes it is also a good idea to get people from other businesses with other experiences. After many months of searching, we hired a Canadian who had worked in Food and Beverage all around the world and had great success. He was high in detail and knew how to drive profit; he was nearly the opposite to Scott, who was very creative. This new CEO was all structure. In fairness, it was exactly what the business needed after a more creative CEO: fresh eyes over the business on ways we could be better and more efficient.

No matter how good a CEO, or any executive for that matter, is, it takes months to get your head around a business. There were a number of things in the businesses that Jeff and I were not that happy with and it was important for us to set up the new CEO for success. We looked at the business with a critical eye and made some hard calls with regard to executive moves. We hired a gun who was from the supermarket world, Claire Lauber, and Jeff enticed a previous employee, Joanne Bradley, whom Jeff believed was the best in the business, back. They were a dynamic team, a perfect mix. In a short period of time the business was once again flying. It drives me mad when people put up with average performance for too long; I have seen time and time again the difference one person in a senior role can make to a business but often people are too scared or busy to make the change.

For the last 10 years, we have always been on the lookout for young and exciting brands. Under the Retail Zoo banner we have Boost, Salsa's and an amazing South Australian brand called Cibo. Retail Zoo is about growth and we needed to find another business for our business.

We absolutely love Noosa and for months there was a vacant spot near the roundabout on Hastings Street. We often wondered what we could put in there. One day a new burger place popped up called Betty's Burgers. It was an instant hit, with lines around the corner from morning to night—this was finally the business we were looking for. Jeff contacted the founder, David Hales, a dynamic and successful guy from Tasmania who had owned and worked in pubs there for years. He has the passion and the drive to understand what it takes to make a successful business. Jeff met with David and started the conversation. After months of back and forth, and many burgers later, a deal was done and Betty's Burgers came under the Retail Zoo banner. This is an incredible brand that has that X factor that you are always looking for. David has gone on to other ventures and will no doubt create another amazing brand. In the meantime we have the pleasure of growing this brand into a leading burger brand in Australia.

With the maturity of the Boost brand and the growth of Betty's Burgers, Retail Zoo had the perfect growth platform to take the business to the next level.

What do I want to be when I grow up?

Boost Juice is a vastly different company from when we started—as it should be. Having now stepped into a director's role, I do miss the dynamics of solving a problem, leading a big team and feeling like you are under fire. I don't miss the legal battles, some of the HR issues and the grind that can in fact break any entrepreneurial spirit.

Like when raising children, there is always a time that you need to pull back—allow new people with new ideas to take the business to the next level.

Boost was all-consuming and it did take me away from my relationship and my kids; I was and probably still am obsessed with the business. Stepping back allowed me to do things like *Shark Tank* and *Survivor*, both of which were extraordinary experiences. I am the eternal student, and getting involved with some of the businesses that we have invested in has that same excitement of the early days of Boost—without the initial pain. Now into my fifties, I have learned so many lessons that I love to share with new businesses that are starting out. My role in Boost is now mentoring and being a director on the board, which allows me the freedom to work out what I want to do when I grow up. With most of the stress of the business now taken out of my hands, I have never felt healthier and had more energy. Riley, who was a babe in arms when I started Boost, works for Retail Zoo now and is a gun in the digital world. Oliver is travelling around South America, having the time of his life (no idea where he got the travel bug from). My oldest son, Samuel, has flown the nest and is married with two of his own children. Tahlia, who is now 11, continues to bring Jeff and I smiles and love every day. All the kids get along and we are very family orientated. I certainly did not win mother of the year, any year in fact, but I must have done something right: all my kids are amazing humans. When people call me successful, I actually think '*I am*'—not because of the success of the business, but because of the love I have for and from my family. Jeff is still and always will be the love of my life: I am a success, because I love and am loved.

Like my kids, Boost will always be a part of me. I am as passionate about the business as I was the day I started. Both Boost and myself are now moving into our new phase of life … and I think both of us will do okay.

The journey continues

Jeff sees Janine today as the best she has ever been—and perhaps the best she ever will be. Jeff says, 'She is totally self-confident; she is at peace with where she has taken the business. She has let others come in and do what needs to be done, she has a beautiful daughter and three sons (who love her to bits), and she has unleashed her high-achieving, obsessive, improvement capacity on the wonderful world of yoga.

'Funny enough, we made a deal at the start of 2012: she would get into horses (which is my obsession) if I would get into yoga (her obsession). The result? We're both now "obsessed" with each other's suggestions, which is great.

'With Janine, I can honestly say what you see is what you get. She is a beautiful woman inside and out. A girl from the 'burbs who worked her guts out, while simultaneously scaring the crap out of herself, to build a new and exciting brand in Australian retail. I have been a very lucky partner to share the journey with her. We made it out the other side stronger and more in love than ever.

'All I can say is *Wow!* what an incredible journey … And you will never meet a better chick.'

PART III

SURVIVING *SURVIVOR* AND BEYOND

With a strong CEO in place, I had more time to be able to pursue other opportunities. *Survivor* was one that I could not pass up; it ticked all the boxes for me. It would challenge me, scare me a little (okay, a lot) and help me see what I am actually made of. Most importantly, it ticked that adventurer box, which I think is what I really am.

The following chapters are about my *Survivor* adventure. It was a life-changing and crazy (like really crazy) thing to say yes to. It is real and raw. I hope you enjoy it ...

8

WHY ON EARTH WOULD I DO *SURVIVOR?*

Before I explain why I would subject myself to the hardest adventure I have ever experienced in my life, I'd better explain what *Survivor* is. *Survivor* is a reality TV show that started in the United States in 2000. It's now up to Season 40 in the US, while the Australian version is only on Season 4. I bring up this point because the American version is only 39 days long, while the Aussie version is 50 days ... 50 days! (You can make up your own mind as to which is more gruelling to film and who are the tougher competitors.)

There is no question that this show is a reality show, but the producers think of it as more of a documentary style. So there is very little 'producing': there are no retakes, no-one gives you lines to do, they simply film you 24/7. The premise is splitting 24 somewhat random people (who have never met), all with various pedigrees, skill sets, ages and talents, into two 'tribes' of 12 and dumping them on an island (in Fiji, in my season) to compete with each other for food and overall survival. The last person not voted off the island wins $500 000. Besides the chance to win the money, it sounds insane—I realise that. Did I mention you only get a few items of clothing, the food you eat is only what you can catch or win, and there are no beds, bathrooms, toothbrushes or shelter of any kind? The camera crew (who are everywhere all the time, 24/7) never offer you a secret hamburger, or stick of gum, or even a wink or a smile.

You battle every day for either a reward or for immunity (not the inoculation kind). The winning tribe of a reward challenge benefits from the rewards, which are either food, necessity or comfort—think a fishing net, knife, chocolate bar or flint. When a tribe loses an immunity challenge they go to 'Tribal Council'. This is where you get mentally abused as your fellow losers decide which of you gets thrown off the island and sent home. Now at this point you're probably thinking 'home' is not such a bad place, and you'd be begging 'please pick me'—but after starving and fighting to win challenges every day, something inside each of these 24 competitors says 'you must win, you must survive'. Whether this desire to subject yourself to the above for 50 days and nights is the true 'Aussie competitive spirit' or insanity, I have yet to decipher. With all of that said … why on God's beautiful green earth would anyone want to be physically or mentally abused like this? So WHY?

The 'why' for each of the *Survivor* competitors is unique. I could never begin to suggest their individual reasons for competing, even though I have gotten to know most of them very intimately. The reason I agreed to be on the Champions Tribe for Season 4 all started in January 2019 at a 'New Year's goal-setting' breakfast. I hold this annually with a few girlfriends, Andi, Sarah and Susie, at my beach house. I know … 'goal-setting brekkie'? I may have already answered the 'why' here.

Every year my beautiful friends and I create five personal goals and five professional goals that we want to accomplish within the year. My goals were pretty interesting for 2019. Retail Zoo was mature and we had an effective CEO so I was moving more into a mentor role than a day-to-day one. I had spent the last 20 years running like a madwoman to get things done; it felt like a real change-of-life goal-setting opportunity. My goals were:

1. Meet some new people (I am a bit of a hermit).

2. Do something that scares me. (The older you get the more cautious you become. For example: I love to surf—but the surf I go in has smaller waves. I love to ride a horse—but now I just trot. When I'm on a rollercoaster all I can think of is, 'When was it last maintained?')

3. Lose some kilos (we always have a rip-roaring summer thus resulting in three to five kilos being put on).

4. Get out of my comfort zone. (I have a nice routine, which works beautifully for me, but I needed to shake it up a bit.)

5. Try something new. (I was feeling I was in a bit of a rut, so I felt like I was ready.)

In writing this, I can sense a pattern here: 'new', 'scary', 'comfort zone', 'get out of routine'. What I did not realise was the *Survivor* gods were listening as well. Not long after I had set these goals, the producer of *Survivor Australia* called and asked if I would participate. I felt physically sick, as deep down, I knew I could not say no.

After hanging up, I immediately thought, 'As if I can take two months out of my life to go play *Survivor!*' Lack of time is pretty much everyone's excuse to not do something—but never a good one. I spoke to Jeff and Tahlia (my 10 year old) and said, 'I have good news and bad news. The bad news is that I may have to go away for 10 weeks.' Tahlia's face dropped. 'No way are you going.' She then asked, 'What for?' I explained my phone call and Tahlia jumped off her chair, threw herself into my arms and said 'You said YES right?' Tahlia is a massive *Survivor* fan (having watched every season of *Survivor Australia*) and could not think of anything she would rather see me on.

I had honestly thought my family would be saying 'Absolutely not, how can we live without you for 10 weeks?' The image I had of my role in this family was so off I had to laugh at myself. With complete family support (from Jeff, Samuel, Oliver, Riley and Tahlia) there was only one person left to convince: me.

I have a super-soft bed. In fact, choosing a bed is one of my superpowers. I get the perfect mattress, pillows and sheets all designed for the consummate night's sleep. I have a seriously gorgeous-looking husband, kids that I really like to spend time with, beautiful friends and an interesting, diverse life. Why give this up to sleep in the elements, with no 1000-thread-count sheets (or even a bed for that matter), to spoon complete strangers for warmth—strangers who will no doubt smell bad and eventually turn on me? The answer is simple ... life is there to be lived!

When starting Boost, we wanted a positioning line (a phrase that would encapsulate our vision) and I kept coming back to my 'Love Life' motto. I wanted to create a business that could help me achieve my 'love of life' as well as helping staff and customers to do the same. 'Love Life' for me was creating a business that could give me the freedom to work the way I wanted to work. It was creating a store, product and staff that could help customers feel that little bit better, with a great-tasting product and real ingredients in a cool environment, all served with a smile. I saw this decision to do *Survivor* as an extension of this motto.

I had worked with the production house Endemol Shine, the producers of *Survivor*, while on the TV show *Shark Tank* for the previous four years. They are a great professional production house, so I knew that I would be in good hands. I also knew that there was not going to be any special treatment (damn) as they take their role of creating strong shows very seriously.

The timing for *Survivor*, however, could not have been worse. Two businesses that were looking at major changes needed significant input from me. I also sat on the board of directors of a separate business that was having major strategy meetings that I could not miss at the time and our house (that I had been building for 18 months) was in its final stages of completion. But how can one say no to this chance-of-a-lifetime opportunity to really see what you're made of?

My agreeing to be on *Survivor* was based out of fear. I'm not going to lie—fear was what drove me when starting a business all those years ago, and it is a great motivator for being prepared. Yes, I am highly competitive and usually in decent physical shape but, admittedly, I'd become softer as I'd gotten older. I kept questioning if I had lost my winning edge with this soft life of mine. The next few days and weeks would tell me.

Filming started in April 2019, but before the competitors left we had to do every physical test known to man to ensure we were not going to die of a heart attack or other unknown illnesses while filming. We had to do a fitness test, blood test, heart test and even a psychological test, all of which I passed with flying colours ... whew.

I truly believe that, if you know in your heart of hearts that you have done as much preparation as possible, if you fail you will have no regrets. My prep started by watching every immunity challenge that I could find on YouTube. I then discovered TEN All Access, which had every *Survivor* series from the start, so I devoured over 100 hours of *Survivor* over the next few weeks. (I am not sure this really helped or made me more fearful.) What I concluded after bingeing previous *Survivor* episodes was that you have to be humble, nice, strong and extremely lucky to NOT get voted out. I'd also observed that when players are the most comfortable is probably when they're going to be voted out.

Additional prep included hours of internet research. One American contestant mentioned a puzzle app that she used; seconds later I was practising a slide puzzle to try and get my brain into puzzle mode. I met with a body and mind expert, Paul Taylor, who discussed techniques and coping skills to get through the mentally harder times and the physical challenges. I increased my fitness regimen and really reviewed my diet, practising a daily 16-hour fast so that my body was good with no food for longer periods of time. I even arrived in Fiji 24 hours earlier and met with a native Fijian who showed me basic techniques on how to find food, build a fire and build a shelter. At this point I didn't look back on what more I could have done to prepare. Upon arriving at Nadi Airport I felt as confident as I possibly could to start *Survivor*. The reality, which I learned on day one of *Survivor*, was that no amount of preparation could have been enough for the experience I was about to have.

What have I gotten myself into?

I know if you're a sceptic you think that a lot of it is for show: surely there's a toilet and shower somewhere, perhaps a Mars bar hidden in a tree? Maybe some reality shows are a bit fake, but not *Survivor*. They take the documentary aspect of this production very seriously.

I arrived at a little resort called Daku Resort, which looked like it was straight out of the 80s. It definitely needed some love. I met my chaperone (who was there to make sure that I did not speak to any other contestants) and with a smile she collected my phone, wallet and passport. I was thinking, 'I guess I can't change my mind at the last minute and do a runner!' For someone like me, who loves to be in control, it was a strange feeling to hand over contact to the outside world. In a strange way, it was quite liberating. I always have the need to be connected: I get back to people quickly, I make decisions even quicker and I am a machine with the amount of work I can get through. When I work, I have my computer, iPad and phone all around me so that I can multitask—so indeed it was a forced liberation.

After giving up any connection I had to family, work and friends, I was taken to my room and given the house rules. I could not leave my room, talk to anyone other than the chaperone (lucky she was nice) and I had to wait, twiddling my thumbs. The production team really did keep us in suspense as we had no idea how many days we were going to be waiting like this for the game to begin. The room was dodgy, the air conditioner only worked sometimes and the food was average, but I was excited for this adventure. I read books, wrote in a diary and tried to enjoy the solitude.

After three days of this my chaperone finally came and got me and said that we were going to shoot the opening scene. I was loaded onto a bus with three other people: Abbey Holmes (the AFLW footballer), Ross Clarke-Jones (the big wave surfer) and Pia Miranda (the actress). We weren't allowed to speak to each other, and I had no idea at the time that these people would end up being critical to my game and become long-term friends.

We rocked up to a swiftly flowing river and were told to jump in, fully dressed, and walk and swim down the river. And 'for God's sake, whatever you do, do not drink the water.' For me that advice lasted five minutes, as I fell in and gulped a massive mouthful of polluted water. I hoped my immune system was up for some serious overtime work. This was the first time that we saw the other contestants: I knew of Steve Bradbury, but really no-one else. We were still not allowed to talk to each other, which is so strange as you feel incredibly rude by not introducing yourself or simply being polite. Welcome to *Survivor*. After walking and swimming up and down the river we were taken back to our rooms to once again wait for the game to begin.

Twenty-four hours later the game was on. Once again we got onto our bus and were told not to talk to each other. Abbey, Pia, Rosco and I simply gave each other polite smiles. We were allowed only what we were wearing and that had to be vetted by the producers to make sure nothing was waterproof (as it's important that we really suffer). Finally, off we went. We were escorted to the beach with the eight other people who made up the Champions Tribe. Some I recognised but most I didn't (I really don't get out much).

The strange thing wasn't how surreal it all was; it was the stranger sensation of thinking about all the things I had to tell people back home, but having no way of doing so. This forced digital detox was exactly what I needed.

The first day

From the beach we were immediately escorted to our first challenge. Nothing like getting the game going quickly. I stood with my new frenemies and found out what was in store. My nerves were at an all-time high and my mind was racing, 'What if I embarrass myself and fail the first time up?' My daughter would be mortified!

The challenge appeared simple: there was a sand bag in the middle of an enclosed sand ring. Starting at the edge, facing a competitor from the opposite team, you simply had to be the first one to get the sandbag, bring it back to your side of the circle and drop it in a marked square. How hard can that be, right? Well, we found out quickly that it is super hard and the Contenders Tribe had something to prove.

TV viewers saw it as first to three, but when we played it was first to six. The producers, we later learned, would need to edit most challenges for 'TV time'. One by one we squared off. Pia, who I found out later was a famous Australian actress, is a small-framed woman of five-foot-two. She competed against a 40-something woman named Sarah Ayles, a tsunami survivor. She was a solid, strong-looking woman who was about 13 centimetres taller than Pia. Pia is tough as guts (as I would soon learn), but unfortunately she did not have weight on her side and found herself squashed by this woman, who was yelling in her ear 'I need this, I am winning', which she did.

When each team had five wins I was up for the decider. *No pressure*, I thought sarcastically, while seriously worried about my first impression. Through sheer determination I dragged the Contender, Casey Hawkins, and the sandbag to my square. I felt I was off to a good start and was (hopefully) looking good for my new tribe. One thing everyone knows on *Survivor* is you need fire for warmth and cooking or your life is miserable. Thankfully we received a reward of food and flint for our first fire at camp.

After the challenge my team returned to our beach and were finally able to properly meet each other. There were faces that I knew and others that I did not. I had recently seen Ross Clarke-Jones's doco, *Storm Surfers*. Having seen the doco I was surprised that Ross was even alive, let alone on *Survivor*! There was ET Ettingshausen, the NRL champion, whom I did not recognise. (Being from Melbourne, if you are not AFL then you do not exist in sport.) There was a beautiful blonde who I recognised: Abbey, an AFLW footballer. Others included Steve Bradbury, who we all know as the 'last man standing'; the extremely well-known and respected Nova Peris, who is an ex-Olympian; and an exceptionally happy-looking woman who I discovered was Pia Miranda, who had starred in the movie

Looking for Alibrandi. Simon Black, an amazing AFL football player, was in our tribe, along with Susie Maroney, who set ridiculous records in long-distance swimming. Luke Toki I recognised from Season 2 of *Survivor.* Anastasia Woolmer I did not recognise, but later found out was a memory champion. Last but not least was David Genat, a supermodel, who on day one looked quite intimidating. These 11 people were going to be either my best friends or my worst enemies over the next few weeks.

After a few uncomfortable hugs we got onto the matter at hand: building a shelter. It was getting late in the afternoon and the sun set at about 6.30 pm, so we did not have much time. ET and Blacky (Simon Black) took control and started building the shelter while others worked on the fire and food. Nova was self-designated cook (you do not mess with Nova and her cooking) and the rest of us were worker bees. After a lot of hard effort the shelter was done; we were about half a metre off the ground, with a bamboo floor and a decent roof, and were pretty chuffed with ourselves. The fire was going and the rice and beans were in the pot; life was looking okay.

We then got down to the business of getting to know everyone. After this initial 'who's who in the zoo' it was getting late and we started to think about bed. (I use the term 'bed' loosely as it was more like dirt and sand with lots of bugs.) Abbey and I quickly realised we had something in common: we loved to go to bed early, so we hit the sack.

Now, this is where *Survivor* started to feel real. We laid down on the hard, round and ridiculously uncomfortable bamboo. I found a spot that was at least not painful and started to rest—(to call it sleep would be a stretch). Slowly, one by one, the tribe started to join us—and then slowly, one by one, the tribe started to find alternative places to sleep. Steve found a cave, while the rest found somewhere on the beach or in front of the fire. No-one got any sleep night one; we decided to pull the base of the shelter off and start again. We learned that sleeping on the sand with some palm fronds would probably be a better option than on hard, round bamboo. We had just learnt our first lesson on *Survivor*: nothing is as easy as it seems.

On the morning of day two, we were awake and back being busy bees, sorting out things like wood for fire and coconuts and papaya for food, and starting to form relationships with our fellow tribe mates hoping to see if we could form any allegiances. My strategy was to see if I could make some true relationships and form some close bonds that would get me deep into the game. I started with Anastasia, as we have Ashtanga yoga in common, and Pia, whom I immediately liked upon first meeting.

We were all going slow and steady—perhaps a bit *too* slow and steady, as Steve Bradbury was off creating a seven-person alliance called the 'sporting alliance'. Unfortunately (or maybe fortunately), being the 'businesswoman' of the group, I was left out of Steve's alliance, along with a supermodel, an actress and a former *Survivor* player.

Survivor gets real

We rocked up at our first immunity challenge and I was nervous as hell. My strategy was to not be the weakest in the challenges in the early days so I wouldn't be voted off for being a poor performer, but also to not be the strongest, so after the tribes merged I wouldn't be seen as a threat. It was so important that I gave it my all so that I could prove myself. We walked into the challenge and Jonathan LaPaglia, the host, said 'Come on in' (which he says a lot), as if welcoming us into his home and not a scary challenge that could potentially end my game or my life (which I thought may be the case at times).

The stakes were high: the losing team would have to go to Tribal Council and vote one of their members off. This happens after each immunity challenge until there are only a few players left. Then a jury (made up of players who'd been voted out) votes for the winner, who gets to take home a nice little tax-free cheque of $500 000 (and bragging rights for life).

The challenge started with an obstacle course. We had to throw ourselves over three large poles, drag a seriously large wooden object across the field, lift it up, climb up a ramp and jump down some holes. The last stage was up to the two people we selected to throw the hammer at a target. (I often look back at these challenges and wonder at all the ways we could have been injured, but at the end of the day, when Jonathan said go, we'd go!) The Champions were the fastest to get to the end of the course but unfortunately it came down to the hammer throw, and we'd made the stupid decision to put up a speed skater and a model to do the throw when we had footballers and other sportspeople who would have been better suited. It cost us the game and the Contenders beat us. Nova was not happy. She'd put her hand up for throwing, as she is an A-grade cricket player, and potentially could have been better than David and

Steve (as would have Simon and ET), but that is sport. We completely supported each other in defeat. But we still had to return to camp and actually vote one of these virtual strangers off the island.

We returned to camp and started to scramble. At this stage, I had no idea that there was a 'sporting alliance'—I thought people were still working it out.

Luke, who plays a great social game, was getting to know people and I was suss of him as I knew he was a good player. I immediately liked Ross and knew he was a good guy and I thought I could trust Anastasia. I was starting to get to know David, and, like with Pia, I immediately got on with Abbey, so I thought we might have a potential group of seven people. But in *Survivor* you actually never know who is with you until you read the votes.

Pia, Abbey, David and I went to the well with Luke to discuss the vote, and he suggested Ross because he was pretty noisy at night. As the group was talking, Nova walked up to us and I made a near fatal move by putting Susie's name out. (My reasoning being that on a 'Champions Tribe' they would want to keep the team strong. Despite the fact that Susie is an incredible athlete and has achieved things that hardly anyone on the planet can, she was not an all-rounder and not strong on the ground. She lost her first reward challenge and she was clearly the weakest in the first immunity challenge.)

My strategy going in was to keep a low profile, not put names out and go along with the numbers to see the lie of the land, but what do I go and do? I wait until there are a bunch of people around and throw Susie's name out there, without considering who might have made an alliance with her. I noticed that when I said Susie's name, Nova said nothing and just gave me a look. I got used to that look as she was not a fan of mine, which she made very clear over the coming days.

Strategy blown. I was thinking—*Bugger … I may be going home day one.*

The day went on with lots of names going around, and I was told to vote for Pia. Despite really liking Pia from the start I was so concerned that the next name might be mine that I decided to vote with the numbers.

How the production works is that we'd get back to camp after a challenge and we'd have about three to four hours (depending on when the challenge finished) to talk and work out who to vote off. Then the production crew would call 'lockdown': this meant that we were no longer allowed to talk, look at each other or gesture to each other in any way. It was like we no longer existed to each other. Lockdown lasted until we were actually sitting at Tribal Council. In fact, we'd even get blindfolded in the van on the way to Tribal so that there were no last-minute plans. The production team take the game and the rules very seriously. By the time lockdown was called, I thought Pia was the one we were voting out. I did not know that there was a plan forming and that Nova wanted Anastasia gone because she was annoying her. *Survivor* lesson number two: don't mess with Nova.

The first Tribal Council

We arrived to our first of many Tribal Councils. This is where we got the famous torches and were told that 'fire is our life': when Jonathan snuffs out the fire, you go home. We all sat on a log in the order we were directed to. Where we were sat ends up being very telling, as they make you sit with your alliance. I think they do this so that it makes it easier for you to talk during Tribal Council. It also ends up being a bit of a giveaway as to who was on whose team. At this stage we also discovered for the first time that those bloody logs are the most uncomfortable stools on the planet.

I was sitting next to Luke, who I was starting to get really fond of (that is his superpower). Jonathan started asking questions and Luke leaned towards me and whispered, 'Are we still voting for Pia? How do you spell it?' I laughed, said yes, shook my head and told him he'd be fine. We got up one by one and cast our votes, telling the *Survivor* gods (better known as cameras) why we voted that way, and then returned to the torture stools.

No matter how many times I sat at Tribal Council, through Jonathan slowly calling out the votes, I was always nervous that the vote was me. He read out three votes for Pia ... then all the rest were Anastasia. This was my first blindside: when you think that everyone is voting one way and you are in the minority who is voting another way. In other words, you are on the bottom of the tribe.

Returning at night after a Tribal Council is always interesting; there is a level of discomfort, as everyone now knows where everyone stands. For me and Luke the news wasn't good.

When we got back to camp Pia came up to me and thanked me for not voting for her. There was an uncomfortable silence, then I came clean and admitted that I actually had. We both laughed and Pia said she would have done the same; she understood that the first vote is really 'anyone but me'. From that time onwards, I knew the only time I would write her name down would be for the win if she got there.

Going to sleep that night I knew I had a lot of work to do.

A win and a loss

All the challenges are scary and intimidating, but I found the pressure of the reward challenge a little less as it didn't determine whether your tribe went to Tribal Council. Still, turning up to our second reward challenge was daunting. We rocked up and saw a round sanded area with a huge timber structure that turned in the centre (like the hands of a clock). A large post expanded out to the edge of the circle that we had to push on, in pairs, at the same time as a pair of Contenders, moving the timber around with all of our strength to step over the winning line first.

We started with our biggest boys and they lost. Up next were me and Abbey. Deep down I was happy to be positioned as the second strongest woman in our tribe. Abbey and I were a great team; she is a sporting superstar. I learnt quickly that there are two Abbeys: one is sweet, kind and wouldn't hurt a fly, and the second is 'game face Abbey' who is fierce and you had better try your best to win or watch out. I personally like 'game face Abbey', as she is extremely motivating, and we won our round. Each pair came and went and eventually the Champions were victorious.

The team arrived back into camp smiling like Cheshire Cats. Our cockiness was short-lived, however, as we lost the next immunity challenge. Suddenly it was my head on the block.

The sporting alliance was strong and they were very confident in themselves. My group was Luke, David, Pia and me; we needed Abbey and Rosco to flip so that I did not go home. We had to use all of our collective strengths and persuasive powers to make sure I did not go home. We certainly had the team to do it. Luke has incredible powers to convince people to do what he wants and knows the game better than anyone; Pia with her acting skills was convincing; and with my powers of persuasion I thought we had a real chance of converting Rosco and Abbey to our side. Rosco is one for his word, and he'd told me early on that he would not write my name down and I told him the same—so really it was just Abbey we needed to get across the line.

In my opinion the Champions were acting like a losing team by not keeping their strongest players, and I said so in my speech at Tribal Council. Nova was playing the blame game, which for me is the opposite of how Champions work. Luckily for me we got the numbers for the night and I got the joy of sleeping another night in the dirt. Did I mention that it rained that night? I was cold, wet and hungry, yet thrilled to still be in the game!

The tribe swap

If you watched the show you would have seen our alliance of players— Luke, David, Abbey, Rosco, Pia and me—were able to get Steve and Nova voted off before they got us. We also managed to do pretty well on the tribe swap. I remember during the swap being incredibly nervous, as all your hard efforts and prior negotiations can go out the window with the luck of the draw.

I was relieved to see that Abbey, Pia, Simon, Rosco and I had all pulled out the pink buff, becoming Contenders, and was also thrilled to see that we got 'The Horse' (Shaun Hampson)—I believed he was the main reason the Contenders were winning most of the immunity challenges. I also believed that I would work with Shaun long term, as he is one of the nicest guys you can find, and a real game player—which was what we were all there for.

The new Contenders team was Rosco, Abbey, Simon, Pia, Casey, Matt Farrelly, Harry Hills and Shaun; we had the majority and, to top it off, I had secretly found the Contenders immunity idol a few days earlier and could play it if needed. (Immunity idols are small objects hidden near the campsites. In our season, there was a Contenders idol hidden in the Champions camp, and vice versa. Whoever found one of these idols could only play it at Tribal Council to cancel out the votes against them when on the tribe the idol belonged to. My decision to hold the idol for an 'insurance policy' paid off—you get lucky sometimes!)

Photograph by Nigel Wright.

Our first win as the new Contenders team was the café reward. This is when I started to feel differently about David. Abbey, Pia and I realised that David was playing hard and not necessarily on our side. In my opinion he committed four mortal alliance sins:

1. Put out the name of one of your alliance (Pia).

2. Name one of your alliances as the 'power couple' (David told me the two of us were the power couple).

3. Promise one of your alliance members to go to the end with them (Abbey).

4. Think women don't talk ... (David, really??)

Now, of course, this is *Survivor* and lying is part of the game. But so is trusting your alliance—and if you do lie, you have to be pretty careful no-one will find out. Once we found that David was playing us, he was target number one.

But *Survivor* is complex; we knew we could not trust David, but we also knew we needed him as a number after the two teams merged. The best way to do this was to make David a mutual enemy to Shaun and us.

While on the Champions beach David made up a fake immunity idol. As I had found an idol, I had all the paperwork that he would need to wrap the fake idol in to give to someone in the future. As mentioned above I'd found the Contenders idol. Shaun had found the Champions idol. When David realised this, it was his chance to finally use his fake idol and get an idol of his own. During one of the challenges David swapped Shaun's idol with the fake one; unfortunately Shaun never opened the package, so he never discovered it was fake. For us, it was easy: we simply told Shaun that David gave him the fake idol and then watched him go for David. Oh dear, men are so simple. (If you're a man, I am joking … ish.)

We hoped that this would get Shaun to trust us and potentially be a number after the merge.

Photograph by Nigel Wright.

But I digress—what we did not anticipate was the *Survivor* gods throwing us a curve ball when suddenly Shaun was moved to the Champions Tribe.

This was good and bad for us. Good that they did not take one of us (former Champions), which would have weakened our numbers. Bad as it made us a weaker tribe physically, and it also prevented us from continuing to develop our relationship with Shaun further.

Despite losing the very powerful Shaun, we won the next challenge. Simon is a seriously talented sportsman; he was basically my coach and I listened to every word he said before each challenge.

This challenge was simple: someone had to dive under the water and pull a rope to keep a wooden trapdoor open while another member threw a ball through the opening; once the person could not hold their breath any longer, the opening would close. Simon was incredible on the throwing, and of course Rosco can hold his breath for, in his words, 'as long as it takes'. We truly smashed the challenge, earning a night off from Tribal Council.

We did not know what was happening in the other camp; we knew David had an idol and I was sure Luke did too, but when we rocked up at another challenge after their Tribal Council David and Luke told us that they had used their idols and that they were seriously screwed without our help.

With the game of *Survivor*, you always have to protect yourself from the next vote, but also look ahead to after the merge (when all the contestants merge into one tribe). Former Champions were the majority in my current tribe; David and Luke were in the minority on the other tribe. We needed to keep David and Luke safe if we could so that when we got to the merge the former Champions would be in the majority. It's all about being on the right side of the numbers. Our alliance had a long conversation about throwing the next challenge, so we could vote out a former Contender on our tribe. We were all competitive but this was *Survivor* and we had to outwit, outlast and outplay.

Despite the fact that David was no longer as trustworthy at that point, he was still someone who could get us further through the game. Every single one of us came to the conclusion that we had to throw the next challenge as we had the numbers in our tribe, and Luke and David did not.

In my opinion you cannot think one Tribal Council in advance; you need to think three or four moves ahead and make decisions based on this.

With our boys protected for another day we went to work out how to get rid of Harry, and with another immunity loss we had our shot. Casey was playing hard and going from Harry to us; she was hard to trust but she was also smart and she knew we had the numbers. I thought she would vote with us despite the fact that Harry told her he would play the idol for her. At the end of the day, Harry got the majority of the votes but with him playing the idol Casey went home.

Afterwards we had days to get to know Harry and Matt, and they are both genuinely good guys. At first, I was not sure of Matt, as he was all huff and puff at the challenges. But when you get to know him, he has strong character: he is a schoolteacher and someone that I thought I could work with. When we lost yet another challenge, it was Harry that we wanted to go … again.

Photograph by Nigel Wright.

As you can imagine there was a lot of running around, particularly with Rosco following Harry around 24/7 to make sure Harry didn't find another idol. I am sure neither of them slept a wink. We now had the numbers to be able to split the votes. We would vote Harry off and Matt was the split vote; in other words, either Harry or Matt was going home. We were sure that Harry could not possibly have another idol, but just in case, Matt was our number two. Tribal started like it always did, with Harry playing the nice guy, while Matt was surprisingly aggressive. Once we went to vote, to our surprise Dirty Harry, the cockroach, once again survived another day. He played yet another idol.

Challenging times

The next reward challenge was one of the most confronting challenges that I did on the island.

Once again the challenge was at the tower of terror, with a plank that went out over the water. I am not really scared of heights but the idea of being blindfolded on a plank did not really rock my boat.

Abbey hates heights and Pia is not a fan either, so I went first out of the girls. They blindfolded me and walked me out to a spot where I stood for what seemed like hours while Jonathan was announcing the challenge.

We had to untie a rope and throw a ring in the water, then swim to the hook: the person who hooked their ring first won. I did okay; I untied the rope and was in the water quickly. Baden Gilbert however, got the ring on the first shot and I lost, which meant the reward was lost. (Did I tell you that I hate losing? I really hate losing.)

The immunity challenge was next, and it was in an area that was full of mud.

The mud was seriously up to your calves and you could barely walk, but when Jonathan says go, you do not think; you just do. Down the slide I swallowed a mouthful of muddy water, then, with a mallet in hand, I got to take all my frustrations out on a plank of wood. I have to say it actually felt really good.

Photograph by Nigel Wright.

Even though we had more women than men in our team we got to the end quicker and we were up to the puzzle first.

It was no secret that Harry was next on the chopping block so we thought it was fair that he had a chance at the puzzle, which he said he was quite good at and he was highly motivated to win.

Despite the fact that one member of the other tribe was trying to throw the challenge, we lost. Once again I got the pleasure of sitting on those really hard bits of wood at Tribal Council.

I have to admit, I was really starting to like Harry—he has the most amazing recipes in his head and a very cheeky smile—but this was a game and it was Harry that we wanted gone as we trusted Matt just that little bit more.

Later that night at Tribal Council Harry 'Houdini' pulled a rabbit out of the hat with another hidden immunity idol, and Matt went home.

One thing I liked about the people in my tribe was that they knew it was a game. So when we returned to camp it was pats on the back to Harry, and off we would go, plotting his demise or him plotting mine.

After this time I started thinking that maybe we actually needed to work together. If we could not eliminate Harry, then working with him might be the answer.

9

SURVIVOR CONTINUES

At the Contenders camp we knew that we were very close to merge, but in *Survivor* there is nothing predictable, so we were unsure if we had one or two more days.

I had played my idol the night before, even though it turned out I didn't need to because my name was not written down. I still believed it was the right thing to do: my idol power expired after merge, so I only had two more Tribals to play it. I'd decided that if Harry played an idol then I would play mine, since with his votes cancelled out the odds of me going home was significantly higher.

Going into the last challenge I was unprotected. I have to say it was very nice to have that little necklace in my bag, even if it was the skull of a dead animal!

We arrived at another immunity challenge. We had to jump across logs that stood out of the ground, from half a metre to about 1.5 metres in height—which was a long way to fall. The distance was such that you had to jump from log to log. The million ways I could hurt myself on this challenge ran through my head. My fear was nothing compared to Pia's, who being only five-foot-two, was really nervous about how to get across without serious injury.

Photograph by Nigel Wright.

With these challenges it is just as much a mental game as a physical one. Pia told herself that it was nearly impossible, so it became impossible. Pia fell 10 times until she sprang across the poles like the dancer that she is.

We all made it across but we were miles behind. The next part of the challenge was the easy part—a simple swing across a small gap—when it all went pear-shaped.

Photograph by Nigel Wright.

When it was Rosco's turn, he swung and suddenly the rope somehow detached from the top. We weren't sure if it broke or the rope untied, but the result was the same: Rosco was in a ditch with some serious damage to his foot. This was devastating to me. When you are having this experience, you know it's a game but that doesn't take away the feelings and relationships that have evolved with your teammates.

When it was freezing at night, Rosco would be the one to give you his jumper. He was the one who did the fire, and he never ever stopped working. He was the one who made us laugh and would not take anything seriously. He made the camp fun. When he got injured it was the first time in the whole experience that I actually cried. I cried tears of frustration and anger—most of all, I was going to miss him if he had to leave. We did not know at the time if the injury was serious enough for Rosco to go home; we had to keep playing and prepare for who to vote off.

Harry had proven that he could find idols. Even though we thought the chances of him finding another idol was slim, if anyone could, it would be Harry. So even though logic said Harry should go home, we needed to split the vote. And we knew that whoever's name was written down, they would never trust us again after the merge.

Rosco, Abbey and Pia were my first alliance, and we'd had to fight our way to get where we were. Simon was part of the original sporting alliance and, even though I loved Simon and wanted him on my team, there was no way I could put down the name of any of my original alliance members.

When Casey was there, she had told us that Shaun was trying to get Simon to go over to his side and that Simon told him that he would consider it post merge. We also knew that if we put Simon's name down as a split vote then he would know that he was on the bottom of the alliance and would definitely go over to Shaun at merge. Harry and Shaun were enemies, so we thought Harry could be a number for us at merge and would be less likely to move to Shaun's team than Simon.

Pia and I agreed, and Abbey could see that we had no other choice. We just had to talk to Rosco when he came back from getting his foot treated. We were not entirely certain which way he would go. Sadly, and with great frustration for all of us (but fortunately for Simon), Rosco did not return to the game.

Photograph by Nigel Wright.

With the new morning also came a major milestone in the game: MERGE!

In *Survivor* there were a number of milestones that I had wanted to achieve:

1. Not being the first voted out.

2. Making it to the tribe swap.

3. Making it to the merge.

The next milestone would be making the top three. After all the close calls and crazy challenges, I was thrilled we made the merge, especially considering Pia was nearly voted out day one and I was in the same position on day three.

We were all rapt to make this step, but I was not prepared for how crazy it got. I am a really logical person and my superpower is making complicated things simple. For me and my team, getting to the top five was simple if we kept our heads and kept to the plan. But before we were able to merge and go back to our original camp, we had one more challenge to face.

I always laugh when people say to me, 'Oh they must give you handouts or something for comfort.' This is so far from the truth, even to a point that they make it harder for you. But we all knew what we signed up for. An example of this raw torture was the next reward challenge: we each had to hold a bag that was 5 per cent of our body weight over our head. I was disappearing from weight loss so my bag was relatively light, but it was still bloody heavy to me. We simply had to drop the bag if we wanted a temptation item. What viewers didn't know is that 24 hours before this challenge both tribes, who were already very hungry, ran out of food. Having a food challenge was smart television as we were all highly motivated to eat. Daisy proved to be incredibly strong on this challenge, and her reward was a box with all the temptation items in it as well as an idol.

After the reward challenge finished I was so happy to be walking back to my old camp as part of the merged tribe; it felt like coming home. Our original tribe was very practical; we had made a good shelter and camp. The other camp was not as good and it was ridiculously windy on that side of the island.

Here we were, six of the original Champions and six of the original Contenders. From the Champions we had Pia, Abbey, Simon, David, Luke and myself. On the Contenders tribe we had Shaun, John Eastoe, Daisy Richardson, Baden, Andy Meldrum and Harry. It was a great effort by all, and my alliance had only lost Rosco (from an injury, not Tribal Council). To come from 11 Contenders and seven Champions when the teams were re-shuffled to six of each was a great start to the merge.

Shaun, rightly so, was concerned about the even numbers. He was talking about sticking strong with his Contenders, even if it meant drawing rocks. (This is what happens if a vote is tied; the people who have been voted for draw rocks randomly from a bag to decide who goes home.)

The Champions were not in a great shape. Shaun had just won the immunity challenge and we were convinced that Daisy had an idol from her reward, which put them in a strong position to tilt the scales to the Contenders' side.

Luckily for the Champions everyone disliked Andy, and we managed to convince them that getting rid of a Contender was a good idea. Luke promised Shaun that they would even out the numbers at a later date. This never happened and the Champions maintained a strong team for the next few votes. We were not going to give away our advantage. The reality was that with Andy gone the Champions were, for the first time, in the majority.

When you make the merge, everyone goes a little crazy. This was made clear on 'the merge night' episode. People were anxious to make big moves, even if it was to the detriment of their own game.

The immunity challenge was up next and David did an amazing job beating Shaun. Finally, we had a free shot at taking Shaun out—then the *Survivor* gods threw in yet another twist. Instead of going back to camp, they set up three camp fires around which we could talk. This was ingenious on their part as it caused confusion, doubt and fear. The only one standing in the same spot was David, with the immunity necklace around his neck.

Photograph by Nigel Wright.

It was when we were at the end fire that Shaun threw out the idea of voting for Luke. Simon was keen for a scalp, as was Pia. Suddenly I found myself agreeing to a vote of six people voting out Luke. At that moment no-one had time to think things through; I hate making calls on the run, as it generally makes for bad decision making.

Things moved very quickly after that and as soon as we said yes to voting out Luke, we were all separated again. There was no time to sort out the mess I had just made for myself.

The decision to vote out Luke was stupid. First, Luke was more likely to vote with me than Shaun going forward, and second, Abbey did not know the plan so she would probably flip to another alliance and would never trust us going forward. Meaning Simon, Pia and I would go from the top four of the Champion alliance to the bottom three of the Contenders. Third and most important, we might never get another shot at Shaun as he was the 'challenge beast'.

Since we went straight to Tribal, I had to convince Simon and Pia publicly, at Tribal, that voting for Luke over Shaun was a seriously bad idea. Luckily they listened and Shaun became the first member of the jury.

A note on Shaun: he is a great player and was a good mix of brain and muscle. When he was around, the Contenders listened to him; he could rally them. Without him they were an easier target. I enjoyed playing with Shaun and anyone would agree that he really is a super nice guy.

The blindside

With Shaun's departure, all of us thought we had a bit more of a chance in the challenges.

Pia and I were as close as ever, with Abbey, Luke, David and Simon as our strong alliance. This left Daisy, Baden and Harry as the final Contenders. We did not trust David but he was still a number ... for now.

The next reward challenge was to win a car. It was an endurance challenge: we had to stand between two poles on tiny wooden pegs, and it was torture on the feet. I'd lasted one hour but, looking over at Abbey, I thought she did not look like she was going anywhere. I just could not take it any longer, so off I went to sit next to Pia.

Pia and I watched Abbey and were so impressed by her fortitude, her mental and physical strength, that Pia leaned over to me and said: 'She has to go.'

I always thought that Pia was a more ruthless player than me. I was more methodical; I would think ahead on the moves and try my hardest to execute them in a way that we always had the majority. It had worked for us to this point.

At this stage Abbey was a trusted ally and I was not ready to get rid of her, but Pia was correct: Abbey was a threat that we needed to consider voting out — later.

A side note on Pia—she is the best social player on *Survivor*. Pia has incredible intuition about people and was always accurate in her assumptions, to the point that if she said something was wrong, I simply took it as fact.

Abbey won the car, and off she went with David and John for the reward. The purpose of the rewards was to separate the tribe, so each group gets to plot and plan against the other. I was happy that there were no major changes in the dynamics of the group when they returned.

For the next challenge we had to dig into designated areas to find a set of balls in a bag. The balls were then used to complete a balance puzzle. Digging was intense and exhausting.

You have to remember that in Fiji the challenges were often as rough as they can get—a heck of a lot tougher than what you see on TV. For example, as I was digging my holes, I had to navigate additional obstacles of barbed wire, poles and rocks. This is one of the things I love about *Survivor*: it is raw and real, with no apologies for what you have to endure. Unfortunately, I did not find my balls and Luke took home the necklace.

This was our chance to blindside David. Luke had told me and Pia that David was gunning for us (although Luke may have made this up). We discovered earlier that David was lying about pretty much everything, so we could no longer trust him. If we didn't get him out now he would come for us—and soon.

At this stage of the game, even if David had gone, we still had the majority. We had a strong suspicion that David had an idol so we needed him to feel as secure as possible so he wouldn't play it. David was a confidence player and we needed to make him feel loved and adored. Our plan was to keep the votes tight so that only the people who had to know would know. The problem we found was that everyone wanted David out. He was simply too disruptive and unpredictable, always wanting to make big moves. He was also a challenge beast. All of this combined made everyone feel like it could be any one of us at any time.

Tribal Council came and David was blindsided, going home with his very expensive necklace. I'd also like to note here that this was another near miss for Harry. All David had to do was play his idol and Harry would have gone home. Once again, the cockroach survived another onslaught!

Photograph by Nigel Wright.

The 'John vote' at the next Tribal Council was the one none of us expected. We thought it was simple: it was time for Harry or Daisy to go home. The immunity challenge was the plank: we had to balance over water with our feet on one plank and our hands on another, in a downward dog yoga position. This was the first challenge that I saw and thought *I've got this*. The strongest part of my body is my abs, thanks to over 12 years of yoga. Within seconds, however, I discovered this challenge was not about abs at all—it was all about shoulders. My shoulders are strong, but not like my abs; I came up third this time, and Simon took home the necklace.

There was not too much stress back at camp: the Champions knew the plan and we were about to execute it. Until Pia and Luke saw Daisy find an idol. With Harry in Daisy's ear we thought there was a chance that if they played it right, one of the Champions would go home.

The only thing we could do was put it on the person it would be most unlikely for Daisy to play the idol for: John. This is what *Survivor* does: your best-laid plans are often spoilt by the *Survivor* gods. John ended up joining the boys in Jury Villa.

The day everything changed

Photograph by Nigel Wright.

When we rolled up to the reward challenge the next day, I was stoked. It was the pole challenge, which was made for me. Basically, it's vertical Twister on poles, and I scored the perfect partner in Simon.

I am quite lanky and my toes are the same. I've always been able to use my toes to pick things up and they're quite flexible. To pick out a peg with my toes was pretty easy for me, so this challenge was a cinch. Who would have thought my three-inch toes and all their skills would someday win me some food! I was excited (to say the least) to win a spa challenge after weeks of eating very little. The big decision: who should I take with me?

Pia and I had spoken about it earlier and decided that if we won a challenge, we'd always need to split up and have someone at camp. At this stage, however, Pia had not eaten anything but rice and beans for 20 days. She needed a break as much as I did.

I justified the decision by thinking that if I took Daisy along with Pia, it meant we could possibly get her as a number.

The danger was leaving Luke on the island: he was the master manipulator and, even though I thought Abbey was solid, I knew that she was nowhere near as solid as Pia.

The reward was insanely good: there was more food and chocolate than we knew what to do with, and to have a bed and light at night was such a treat.

Upon returning to the camp we all knew it was important that we downplay the reward: every emotion at this point was heightened. A flippant comment can be blown out of proportion, and having a reward like we did could bring out the green-eyed monster in the people who didn't go. Still, we could tell that there was a shift back at camp. But everyone was saying the right things, so I thought maybe I'd got away with this decision to take Pia. (Spoiler: apparently not.)

Photographs by Nigel Wright.

Having watched the show I can now see that Abbey was feeling like a third wheel with Pia and me, and she started to work with Luke. What you did not see was Luke telling Abbey that we had promised *him* final three. This was a massive *Survivor* lie but it worked like a charm. Abbey began to doubt us and think we were plotting against her, and now Abbey was firmly under Luke's wing.

The next challenge was to hold a rubber ball in place over our heads by keeping pressure on the ball in a bicep curl position. The moment I saw it I remember thinking *There is no way I will last a minute, never mind win the challenge.* With these challenges you need to find a technique, and that is exactly what I did. I found a certain angle with my body and I noticed that, because I'd dropped so much weight due to lack of food, my newly protruding hip bones made a perfect place to rest my arms. This did not save the pain in my wrists or take all the weight off, but it helped me go further than one minute.

I knew Simon was struggling near the end of the challenge and I had more in my tank, but when Simon made an offer to drop, who was I to say no? Either way I knew I would win this one; it was just a matter of time.

I have to say, at this point in the game, having the necklace around my neck made Tribal Council actually quite pleasant. I had no idea what Luke and Abbey were planning, but clearly it saved me that night.

Photograph by Nigel Wright.

Exile

Tribal Council that night came with a twist when Daisy, who we'd thought we voted out, was instead sent to Exile Beach. Exile Beach was somewhere totally isolated on the island; you had to build your own fire and shelter, and then compete with the next person who was voted out to return to the game. At this stage in the game we had been on the island for over 40 days. We were all physically and emotionally tired, hungry, cold and over the conditions. Everyone wanted to win, but if you're not going to win, getting voted out and heading to Jury Villa, where there was all the food you could wish for and a warm bed, was actually quite appealing. Going to exile made the worst-case scenario somehow even worse.

As if this wasn't bad enough for Daisy, the biggest storm of the season came through while she was on Exile Beach, without shelter.

Rain was coming into our shelter sideways and we were hit with 80-kilometre winds. The storm was so fierce over at our camp that a cameraman suddenly lost his umbrella, his camera got wet and he couldn't even stand up because of the wind. He stomped around muttering, 'F%ck this, I did not sign up for this shit!' But he got no sympathy from us: we had no wet weather gear, no umbrella and were huddling together to keep ourselves from freezing. All I could think about that night was Daisy. She had no-one to support her, no body heat, no fire, no food. If she'd waved the white flag to signal she gave up, I would not have blamed her. My admiration for her grew that night; she wore her emotions on her sleeve but she was one tough chick. When I did see her next, I gave her a hug and told her how proud I was of her. She did so well.

The next vote was on the next person to go to Exile. Pia was safe as she had won the last immunity; it was the rest of us that were in trouble. Simon was pissed at me for not pushing harder for Luke but, to be honest, I stand by this decision. Luke, for me at the time, was more predictable than Daisy—plus Luke had Abbey in his back pocket.

What you did not see on the show was Simon was gunning for Abbey. I think he was pissed that she didn't vote with us the last time. Simon approached Luke and told him of his plan to vote out Abbey. Once Luke told Abbey, and then Harry and Baden, Simon's future was decided. Pia and I had no idea that it had changed from Baden and we happily voted how we thought everyone was voting.

This is what is so interesting about *Survivor*: it can twist and turn in a hot second and, with people plotting here, there and everywhere, you can go from top to bottom pretty quick. Clearly, Pia and I were now very firmly on the bottom of the alliance.

As Simon went to Exile, Pia and I were left thinking, *Shit. We're in trouble.*

Photograph by Nigel Wright.

The battle

The battle between Simon and Daisy was intense. It was a classic *Survivor* challenge: they needed to balance a disc on a long stick and navigate the stick through a maze without touching it. If the disc fell you started again. This was repeated until 12 disks were stacked. This challenge was more about being precise than being fast. You would think Simon would have it in the bag, but Daisy was so close. In fact, they both had at least 10 attempts at getting the balance right only to have each one fall down. By the tenth time both were being super careful but in the end they just could not get to the 12. They went to a time-based challenge in which the one who got the most blocks in 10 minutes would win. This was even more intense. You had to decide: only do seven or eight blocks and hope the other drops theirs, or do you try for the 12? Simon was victorious in the end and he returned to camp. Suddenly we had a new Simon: a very angry, determined one.

While the old Simon had always been a polite, incredibly loyal guy who really struggled with the lying part of the game, this new Simon was fierce and wanted revenge. He fought hard when he came back into camp, trying to pull together an alliance to change the outcome, but he just could not do it. His only hope was to find an idol.

Simon found an old clue that Harry and Luke left out saying there was an idol underground, near a palm tree. He was digging for hours (I'm talking 12 to 15 hours) to find this idol; he was not going without a fight. Unfortunately for Simon, all that effort was in vain: the clue had been a fake. His fire went out that night.

Letters from home ...

Photograph by Nigel Wright.

As I'm sure you've noticed, I am very pragmatic in real life and that was evident on the show. I thought ahead, used my social skills to help keep people together to form a strong alliance, and I did not let things worry me (on the surface anyway). I was focused and disciplined in my approach on *Survivor*. I also put my emotions in a box and dipped into them only when I needed to. That was before the letters from home.

On day 42 we were doing our normal routine in the morning and were told that there was tree mail. Now, it can get boring on the beach, so this was the highlight of the day. The tree mail told us two every exciting things:

1. There was food up on the beach.

2. We had letters from home.

I am a real family person, and my husband is my rock and the love of my life. But, like all couples, we had started to take each other for granted. You get annoyed at the little stuff and your iPhone or computer start to seem far more interesting than the people around you. When I left for *Survivor* my husband was spending three to four days per week at the farm that we have on the Surf Coast of Melbourne (this is his happy place, where his horses are) and I was busy in Melbourne.

There was nothing wrong with our marriage, in fact it is far better than most, but we were certainly not being the best couple we could be. While I had no doubt that Jeff would be getting on with anything that happened at home, dealing with the business and helping finish the house that we were building, I did not realise until I had his letter in my hand how much I loved and missed him—and how much he loved and missed me.

We both realised by being away from each other how much we meant to one another, how much we'd been taking each other for granted and how we had started to drift apart.

As you see on *Survivor*, I am not a highly emotional person. I only cried two times: when Rosco hurt himself (which was a big sob) and when I read my husband's letter.

We have been married for over 22 years and I know him well, so just reading the first line I knew that he was struggling without me and that he missed me more than we both thought possible. Reading his letter unlocked all the emotions that I had cleverly kept pushed down and suddenly the floodgates opened. At this stage in the game, I was looking bloody rough and I know that I was a really ugly crier, but nothing could stop the emotion and tears flowing.

Coming home, after *Survivor*, our relationship could not be better. Our love is so strong and our friendship even stronger. I needed him more on that day than I ever needed anyone.

It was very hard once the floodgates opened to contain all those emotions again and continue to play the game, but I had to do just that.

My final challenge

On the day my fire was snuffed out, the sun came up like it did every morning. We had perfected just the right mix of 1/3 salt water to 2/3 fresh water to cook our rice (thanks, Lukie, for that tip) and I could hear the ever-present sounds of coconuts being chopped and the ocean rolling in.

Going into the next challenge, I knew I was in trouble. I knew that I would need to win immunity and the challenge was a ripper. It was essentially an obstacle course challenge that incorporated climbing up a huge wooden ladder that was tangled in ropes, which easily could be twisted. It was a combination of rope management, balance, throwing, and a puzzle, all of which I thought I was okay at.

Jonathan did his 'Survivors ... GO' line and off we went. I was doing well and started to feel confident ... until my rope got tangled!

Photograph by Nigel Wright.

As I unwound myself people were getting further and further away from me. Finally, I got the rope untied, scrambled over the tightrope, then onto the throwing part of the challenge. There was a small target that if you hit it, it moved a pole that was behind it and eventually a key would drop if you hit it enough. With the pressure of trying to catch up, I missed too many throws and was still behind. Finally, I got to the puzzle and off I went, but it wasn't enough and once again I ended up about third. No necklace.

Back at camp we all started our conversations. I have a logical brain, and I simply thought that people would play to get them further in the game: i.e. play for their best interests. Us three girls were the oldest and strongest alliance in the game and, with six of us left, our three votes were the most important and powerful votes in the game. If we got to five votes then we were unstoppable to the final three, so even though Luke was wooing Abbey I still believed that anyone could see the logic in a strong three, not in a strong two.

Abbey was going from Harry to Luke to Baden and back to us.

The conversation that I had with Luke gave me some comfort that he was still with me. Luke is not stupid, and he knew that no-one would want to go to the end with him. Luke suggested voting out Baden, which made sense to me. I knew that it would work for Luke (it would leave Harry, Abbey, Pia, Luke and me, which in Luke's mind gave him a barrier vote of Harry before we would vote out him) and, in fairness, that was my gameplay the whole time: make calls that worked for the best interest of the group or the person I was speaking to. Plus, Baden was a threat to everyone: he was a person everyone would be happy to go to the final two with.

I was about 70 per cent sure I was not going home: voting out Baden was in the best interest of Abbey (strong three), Luke (get rid of Baden and you have Harry as the next obvious vote) and Pia (because I simply loved her and we were tight). So, with logic on my side I thought, *Even though they're gunning for me, their self-interest will prevail.* You are never confident at Tribal, and many times I actually thought I was going home, and this was no different. But it was more intense as I was so close to the end.

Obviously if you've watched the episode you'll know it was not to be for me. My torch was snuffed out. There are always mixed emotions being voted out: on the one hand, you are gutted that you are out of the game and you will not be sole survivor, but having a bed, shower, food and seeing your loved ones is something that you have been hoping for for weeks. It's bittersweet really—I would have taken a hard bit of dirt to sleep on any day to be able to get to the final two.

The second your torch is snuffed you are whisked away by production; it's a whirlwind. They take you to a room with scales and a doctor to see if you are still alive (tick) and then you're asked a lot of questions by the social media team. Apparently, the social media side of *Survivor* is one of the biggest followings in Australia. You are then put in a car and asked more questions and finally you arrive at the resort that is serving as Jury Villa.

I entered Jury Villa very hesitantly. I felt a bit nervous, as I was part of the reason that these other people were sitting there. However, they were a delight: they welcomed me with open arms and we ate a serious feast to fill (or should I say over fill) my belly.

I got to have my first call with Jeff and Tahlia, which was emotional and invigorating. I showered in a real shower, and I slept in a proper bed for the first time in 44 days (other than the night at the spa challenge). I fell blissfully asleep.

We were so lucky with the personalities in the Jury Villa. There was David, Shaun, John, Daisy and Simon, who are all amazing people. The vibe was like a party: the food was plentiful, as was the sun and the atmosphere. It was so very different to living on the island.

I was feeling bad for Pia as we'd been each other's rock for the past 44 days, but I knew her inner strength. She was a fighter; she would be fine, and she had a great chance of winning.

Photograph by Janine Allis.

Before I'd started the show I asked a producer if he had any tips. He said, 'This game can break the strongest. The ones who do well are the ones that see the beauty in every day.'

I thought this was good advice, for both *Survivor* and in life—so I'd done just that.

The beach in front of our camp was not very wide: only about 400 metres from one end to the other. When the tide was out, there is literally no water for about 200 metres, yet even then, it was beautiful in its extremes. Our shelter, the one we'd built on day one, stood to the end and did us proud. (Although the roof couldn't handle much more than drizzle.)

I marvelled at the ways we'd all adapted to our environment. The sun rises about 6.30 am and sets about 6 pm where we were, and we'd quickly learned exactly where the sun would be when it was setting because if you missed it, you were plummeted into pitch blackness with no idea where your gear was.

Rosco had taught me how to look at the weather to try and predict if it was going to rain or not. He always said that he had a 30 per cent chance of being right, but I have to say his accuracy was more like 70 per cent. Being on *Survivor* you rely on nature and the elements to keep you warm and safe. Nature told you what time the sun was setting and rising and many times it made me love being there, whether it was watching a sunset or enjoying a breeze to cool us down. It was such a primal feeling, which I have to say is what made the experience so real and raw.

During the game the sunsets were beautiful, the chatter around the fire was good for the soul, the swimming in the water was refreshing, and all the friendships I made gave me strength and security in the game. There was a lot of good amongst the bad. Obviously there was a great deal of sand and dirt, cold, wet and scary challenges, and manipulation, but when I think of my time on *Survivor*, I seem to only reflect on the laughs and good times.

The friends I made

There are many things on *Survivor* that are hard, but my favourite thing was the hours of getting to know people and the little moments. Here are some of my memories of some of the people.

Harry: In the early days of knowing Harry we did not spend that much time together because I didn't think he was going to be there long. The first time we tried to get Harry out, the *Survivor* gods instead took Shaun. The next time we went for him, he had an idol. Upon returning to the camp that night we laughed. I patted him on the back and thought *I'll get you next time*. The third time (once again) he had an idol and Matt went home. This was our turning point. We laughed together and I started to call him 'the cockroach'. We started to seriously talk about working together, and we would have had to, if Rosco hadn't got hurt.

Pia and I saw merit in working with Harry for many reasons: he was a good game player, he knew when to keep his mouth shut (the hardest thing to find in *Survivor*) and I thought he had a similar game plan to Pia and I. I like Harry, even though he was playing the villain and he wanted the Godmother gone. (This is the nickname that he gave me throughout the game. He wanted the attention off him and on to me. It was fun to embrace the title and it made me laugh.) Harry and I had mutual respect for each other. He's a good guy and I really enjoyed playing with him.

David: I know people either loved or hated David in the game, but David was playing a character and I think he played it so well. He made me laugh so much watching the show. He did not take himself seriously and knew he was there to do a job.

My impression of David when I first saw him was that he was too cool for school. He had a leather jacket (good call), a cap and a strut that was the best I have ever seen. Then he smiled and it turned out he is warm, funny and not stuck up at all.

David was the first person in my alliance, and he is genuinely a good guy. I was thrilled to get to know the real David on the jury and he is a dude. He is funny, witty and very talented. I've told him that I thought he was a tool on the show, which made him laugh. He is also a very talented cartoonist; I hope you get to see some of his work as it's hysterical. I hope we remain friends for years to come.

Rosco: I admit, Rosco was one of my favourites. He was always smiling (other than when he got hurt). He taught me how to find the child within, and he really did look after us. He was naughty; he nearly burned down our camp, he set Harry on fire and was always dropping things on his foot.

He is one of the reasons I loved playing *Survivor*. We've caught up since we've been back home and I will continue to make sure we stay close.

Daisy: I did not have a lot to do with Daisy as she was never in my alliance (other than for a short time in the spa) but my admiration for her is immense. What she went through on Exile Beach, enduring a storm that was as fierce as I have ever witnessed, showed the real character that she had. There is not a bad bone in Daisy's body and I wish her all the best.

John: He was super likeable, funny and did not take life too seriously. He had an incredible work ethic and was never still. I was sad I did not get to spend a lot of time with him on the island, but we made up for it in the Jury Villa. We did a yoga session together while there and he is bloody good at it.

Abbey: I am so fond of Abbey: she is a driven, competitive powerhouse. She will have massive success in life simply because she will make it happen. There are two sides to Abbey: the sweet, soft, emotional side and the challenge beast (who you do not mess with, by the way). I remember in the water football challenge where she screamed at me, 'Go the body J!', which I did, taking poor Daisy down and breaking her top in the process. I loved both sides. I loved competing with her and we were close from day one. I felt very protective of Abbey. We have caught up many times since the end of filming and I love seeing her every time.

Lukie: How can you not love Lukie? That is his superpower: he is so bloody loveable. He was always smiling and cheeky. It does not matter what challenges are in his life, he sees them all as good. He never complained once and was always working, whether that be working with us all with game play or around camp. He is the perfect *Survivor* player. You better be on his side, because if you are not—beware!

Shaun: I did not get to play with Shaun much; we were only together for a few days. When he was around he was a leader people wanted to follow. He had that perfect mix of likeability and intelligence; he knew what was going on and how to change it. I have caught up with him post game with Megan and I hope we continue our friendship.

Simon: I was with Simon the whole time on the island. You will not find a kinder and more loyal man. Despite starving, he always made sure everyone had enough to eat. He was always working around camp and strongly supported his alliance, whether that was the sporting alliance or ours. Simon spoke so fondly about his beautiful wife that I felt like I knew her. I hope to meet her face to face in the near future.

Baden: I only met Baden at merge. He genuinely wanted the best for his tribe. Was he quirky? Yes. Did he love scraping the rice pot? Sure. But his intentions were always the best. I loved getting to know him.

Pia: I saved the best for last. What I was concerned about going into *Survivor* was that I wanted to trust someone, someone who could have my back and I theirs. I found this in a five-foot-two-inch-tall actress named Pia.

We hit it off straight away and she was my sleeping buddy. The area we slept in was smaller than a single bed and it was freezing, so nearly every night I had Pia in my arms for warmth and comfort. We never got sick of each other, we never ran out of conversation and we kept each other sane during the time we were both on the island.

Pia was my moral compass during the game. There were many *Survivor* lies going around, as that is part of the game, but I never once lied to Pia. She was on my team and the plan was always to get to the end together by protecting each other along the way. Pia and I catch up on a regular basis, either in person, or by text or phone. Our daughters are great mates and communicate as much as we do, and I hope that we can do some projects together soon. Pia was my love story in *Survivor*.

The editors

What we actually experienced was a bit different to what you see on TV. You have to remember that the editors need to cut down thousands of hours of footage to 60- or 90-minute episodes that tell a story that makes sense. I am not sure why they did not show more of Daisy on Exile Beach and what she went through or with Simon's fake clue, but at the end of the day something has to go.

There may be some twists and turns to make sure that the story is told well, but the essence of what you see is true and depicts how it happened. The people of *Survivor* take the show very seriously; there are no shortcuts with regard to contestants. They made it tough for us, as it should be. We did it tough and they made no apologies: this is what we signed up for. They also let the game play out with nil to very little interference. I know many of us are quick to assume that certain things are rigged, but this was not the case with *Survivor*; the integrity of the show was always put first.

I personally feel the editors and production team did an amazing job of detailing the story, showing the viewers the game and our raw experiences out in Fiji.

Thanks to Channel TEN and Endemol Shine for having me. I had a ball.

Photograph by Nigel Wright.

Gratitude

There are many lessons to take from being stranded on a deserted island for 44 days, but the biggest is gratitude.

It is amazing how humbling it is to have everything taken away from you. You're forced to see your life more clearly and you become very familiar with the true essence of what gratitude means day to day.

First was my family and friends; I realised that I often take them for granted and am not always present in their company. How could I have ever thought my iPhone or tablet were more important than these real relationships?

Absolute second are the small things we often overlook. Something as simple as flavours: when you have nothing but rice, beans, coconut and the odd papaya it makes food very dull. A door and window, a bed and blanket, a brush (who would I have killed for a brush?), anything to keep you dry or warm: these things are precious.

Competing on *Survivor* was the most humbling experience that I have ever had and one that I am eternally grateful for. This experience has allowed me to open my eyes wider and appreciate everything in my life that much more.

Thanks for reading about my *Survivor* journey; I hope it gave you a bit more insight as to what it was like on a deserted island for 44 days.

I am grateful for it.

PART IV

LESSONS LEARNED WITH BLOOD, SWEAT AND TEARS. LITERALLY.

Being older and (apparently) now wiser, I wanted to share some of what I learned from starting a business with three little kids running around my feet to creating a world-class brand. In the following pages are what I believe it takes to be successful in business and in life. You do not even need to be in business; there's something in there for every reader. Enjoy.

10

WHAT I WISH I HAD KNOWN BEFORE I STARTED YEARS AGO!

As you read from my story, I never did year 12 or went to uni, but I did go to the school of life. Being a traveller teaches you skills you don't learn anywhere else — or not as quickly, anyway. I pride myself on my problem-solving skills and I put that down, in part, to the travelling that I did. You learn to look a little way into the future and see danger before it hits — an invaluable tool in business. When you have only yourself to rely on, you learn to trust your instincts and find resources within yourself you never knew existed.

Lessons from the traveller

Here are some specific lessons I learned in my early twenties that can be applied to many start-up business settings:

- You don't have to put up with upsetting or unlawful behaviour at your workplace, and you shouldn't.

- All people, even the successful or rich and famous, are just people with their own fears, dramas, happiness and sorrows. You are no more and no less than anyone else.

- Some people seem to think that because they have money they need to act in a certain way. Similarly, some women think that to be successful in business they need to act like a man. The most important thing: be yourself.

- If you're ever given a job or an opportunity through someone you know or are related to, make sure you work 10 times harder to prove you are worth it.

- Look at what people do, not what they wear. At Boost and Retail Zoo, we don't have a dress code in the support centre at head office. Having said that, I'm aware that not everybody shares my philosophy, and common sense sometimes needs to come into play. If you have important meetings, dress appropriately. While you might not be judged within your own company, you can't rely on the same attitudes existing outside your business's environment.

Lessons from the early days of Boost

Here's what I learned in my first years of starting Boost:

- Make working *on* your business your priority. Many people who start a new business spend so much time working *in* their business that they never get a chance to grow it.

- You need a fully fleshed-out concept for a brand, and you must provide the whole package for your concept to succeed. You also need a clear, single vision to create something truly special.

- Doing everything by committee doesn't work—if too many people have their say, you end up with a diluted version of the original idea. The store design with our previous business partners was horrible because it was designed by committee. This was an example of my early lack of confidence; I was a pleaser. Have confidence in your vision and let this vision guide you on everything about the business.

- Be resourceful. I do not have a business degree. What I had when I started Boost was the ability to think outside the box, because I didn't know there was one, and learn quickly.

- I knew I could, and would, figure out what was required. I went to great lengths to gain the business knowledge I have now. When people ask me what my background is, I remind them that I didn't go to university, but I had a hell of a teacher—Boost.

- Remain true to yourself and your management style. Two years into running Boost, Jeff sat me down and told me how I should change to become a better CEO. He had strong ideas on what type of person should lead an organisation, and thought I wasn't dealing appropriately with difficult situations. I knew even then that you had to be true to who you are to be a good leader, and told Jeff so. A couple of years later, he told me how proud he was of me for sticking to my beliefs. He acknowledged that his prior advice was totally wrong—that my 'style', which is unique to me, worked.

- Know when to let go and allow people the opportunity to thrive.

- A business's success is all about the people—get the people wrong and it will be detrimental. For example, getting your accounts wrong can cause numerous problems: it's impossible for investors to come into the business if the figures are in question. Making the right decisions within your business is also difficult if you do not accurately know what the business is doing. One of the most important people in any business is the bean counter (okay, the accountant).

- No one person can do it all. The reason that Boost is Boost, and not one of the other juice bars that no longer exists, is the people who I choose to have around me. I think of them as my personal board members. When you get your people right, it makes everything flow. When you get it wrong—get it right quickly!

- It's vital for people who are successful in business to pass on their knowledge to those who can benefit from it. Both Rod Young (our franchising expert) and Geoff Harris did this for me and, in a nutshell, it's why I've written this book.

Integrity: if you ain't got it, you got nothing

These days, people talk a lot about 'integrity' and 'values'. They've become buzz words, used to impress—but do you know what integrity really means? It's true that if your company is known as being one of integrity, you will attract and keep like-minded people—honest, reliable, moral people. Yet ideals often seem to disappear if the bottom line is affected.

The words 'integrity' and 'values' mean nothing if they're not backed up with solid hard work and the right decisions.

So, what is integrity? To me, integrity means always telling the truth and acting in a way that is right for the business, no matter how hard that may be and no matter what the cost. You can't please everyone all the time. Some people may believe you haven't acted with integrity—whether it's an employee you had to let go, or franchisees who think it's your fault they haven't made more money. You can't always help what other people think, but as long as you know you've done the right thing, you can feel at peace. Having true integrity has made Boost what it is today.

The words 'integrity' and 'values' mean nothing if they're not backed up with solid hard work and the right decisions ... To me, integrity means always telling the truth and acting in a way that is right for the business, no matter how hard that may be and no matter what the cost.

Let me give you an example that shows how important integrity is. We had a senior executive in the business who was an amazing talker. When he spoke, his words and tone instilled confidence, and he always seemed to have the answers to all the hard questions. However, this man lacked true integrity—it was all about his ego and making sure that he looked as good as he could. He would often lie and just tell you what you wanted to hear.

As we came to discover, these can be the most dangerous types of people to have in your business, because it takes a long time to realise what they are really like and, in that time, they can do a lot of damage. By the time we uncovered what this man was doing, his area of responsibility was in a terrible condition and we had started to get a high level of resignations—and, worst of all, the culture of the business had changed. Your business's culture is just like fitness—it can take months to get your fitness level up and only weeks to completely lose it. We realised we had (admittedly unknowingly) gone against one of our biggest rules: only hire people with the utmost integrity. At the time this man was hired, we thought he had integrity but we were sadly mistaken. Often mistakes make the business better, and this is true in this case—we now have better systems in place to make sure this does not happen again.

Here's how to act with integrity and ensure it in those around you:

- You can't create a workplace culture of high integrity without hiring people with high values. Be single-minded in seeking out the right staff.

- Always aim to keep your word; if you have to change your mind, be honest about the reason. Be straightforward, accept that you are wrong and don't make excuses.

- Seek consistency between what you think and what you say. People can see through lies, and you cannot fake sincerity.

- Yes, it does sometimes cost money to do the honourable thing. Look at it as a short-term financial loss that can be absorbed. A loss of trust can never be regained.

Motivation — move it or lose it

Recently, a staff member came to me and asked me how to motive the team. I said, 'That's super easy: hire motivated people.' If you surround yourself with people who are looking to you for motivation then you have the wrong people in your business.

Unfortunately, I can't teach you how to find the will to do so but I can tell you that you need all the will in the world to get where you want to go. Motivation, inspiration — call it what you like — is different for each of us.

To succeed, you must unlock that deep personal energy. So, what motivates you? If you can't answer that question, it's time for you to find out. Without that knowledge, you'll never experience the total joy of achievement.

I can't give other people motivation, but I can provide a culture where their achievements are recognised and rewarded in a way that is meaningful to them. When it comes to motivating staff, I look for their 'hot buttons'. For some people, a small gesture is enough — a metaphorical pat on the back when all seems lost. Others may take more convincing and may appreciate incentives, such as time off work or a small gift of appreciation.

I believe that motivation is born from working with great people and achieving great things together. The bigger your purpose, the more fulfilled you'll be at the end of every day.

Many things motivated me on my business journey, but the biggest one in the early years was fear. I had everything on the line: we had sold our family home, all of the cash was in the business and we were renting. Not to mention our home doubled as our office. At 34 years old and with three children, I truly did have everything to lose. There is nothing like putting yourself in this position to give you motivation! The business had to work no matter what so, one way or another, I had to find the solution to every problem.

Fear was there as an underlying factor on the journey but something else also popped up—and that was passion. I found that not only did I love the world of retail and business but also, to my surprise, I was actually quite good at it. My brain worked in systems and in high detail. Whenever something went wrong, my mind immediately went to solutions, and then to ways of ensuring a problem of this type never happened again. Suddenly, the business didn't seem like work anymore—I loved it! And when you love something, motivation to continue is a by-product of the journey.

Passion—love what you do

Having passion is the easiest way to make money, but it's the hardest thing to find. You can teach anything and train anyone, but you cannot instil passion in someone. Passionate people are few and far between. To me, they are like gold. They stand out. People are attracted to them and believe in them; people want to be them and invest in them. Do you have to be loud, extroverted and opinionated to be passionate? No. You can be quietly passionate. This may mean you're overlooked—but not for long. Along with integrity, commitment and a strong work ethic, passion is always recognised.

Having passion is the easiest way to make money, but it's the hardest thing to find. You can teach anything and train anyone, but you cannot instil passion in someone.

So what do I mean by a passionate person? Essentially, passion is tied up with loving what you do. To achieve a goal, you need to throw your heart and soul into it. If you don't, you're in trouble.

When we have a problem at Boost and Retail Zoo, everyone on the team is focused on the solution. Their eyes sparkle with the challenge, and they will do whatever it takes to sort it out — whether it's getting on the next plane or working through the night. When Boost first began, the business took over our lives. Jeff and I were surrounded by work 24 hours a day, seven days a week. That level of commitment gets tiring very quickly if you're not passionate about what you do. When you are passionate, it doesn't feel like 'work'. To be passionate, you need to be doing something that means something to you. You can't fake it. If you do, you won't make it.

I have done an enormous number of media interviews over the past 15 years, and the key thing that I'm often told afterwards is that I ooze passion. When people ask me about Boost, my eyes start to sparkle, my body gets taller and then I'm off — spouting all sorts of information about this business that has been so much a part of my life.

What I also have found is that passion is relatively rare — and so I'm lucky that Jeff has it in spades as well. Sometimes, I would say that a fine line exists between passion and obsession. (These days, when you ask my husband about a horse, his whole face lights up, and he can happily tell anyone who is listening the pedigree of any horse you care to mention.) But this energy and obsession is why others like passionate people and want to be around them — they're addictive and others want some of what they have.

Anyone who has achieved incredible goals has passion, without exception — whether they're a top sportsperson or an amazing musician, passion and commitment are the common bond.

Confidence: tits and teeth

My *Survivor* soul mate Pia had been a ballet dancer when she was young. She always said to me what her mother told her as she went on to perform: 'Tits and teeth, darling!', and off she went to perform. For me, having no tits, I found this hysterical, and now use this for fun. If you are not feeling confident then at least with tits and teeth you look the part.

Self-doubt is your greatest enemy. Confidence is everything. If you believe in yourself, others will believe in you too. Even if you have doubts, hide them! Your confidence is your shield — it will protect you and your team from that highly contagious disease known as defeat. (This is different from pretending you have all the answers when you don't—something I would never recommend.)

Self-doubt is your greatest enemy.

Confidence is everything.

If you believe in yourself, others will believe in you too.

Here are some tips for building your confidence:

- Having the confidence to use your knowledge is critical. Knowledge is pointless unless you can back it up with decisive action.

- Confidence is contagious. I focus on solutions—solutions that my staff believe in. Their belief means they also catch the 'I am, I can' attitude.

- Instil confidence in others through delegation. Make sure they feel your total trust and support. Give them the tools they need to complete the task and ensure they have all the knowledge they need. Allow them the space to ask questions without losing face if they don't know something. Make yourself into the kind of boss who inspires loyalty and hard work—your staff members will naturally feel that they don't want to let you down.

- Confidence is everything in a team because it eliminates uncertainty. If people in management are insecure, it will suck the confidence out of those around them. You will know people who lack confidence by the following traits:

  - they hold onto power by not sharing their knowledge with colleagues and staff

  - their moods are as changeable as the weather

  - they lack communication skills (which leaves their colleagues wrong-footed most of the time)

  - they manipulate and/or turn people on each other

  - they find it hard to make decisions and they may out and out lie.

There are varying degrees of this behaviour, but if someone is guilty of these traits, you have no choice other than to remove them. Remove people like this quickly, because they do enormous damage that can take months to repair. These insecure behaviours are like cancer in your organisation.

- People who feel good about themselves have confidence.

- Here is a simple exercise to boost self-confidence and build a positive team environment. Get your people together and have everyone write their name at the top of a sheet of paper. Hand the papers around, and ask everybody to write an affirmative statement about the person whose name is on the top of each sheet. Each person ends up with a list of positive attributes. As an extension, you can have each sheet framed and presented to your team members. On those 'all too hard' days, they will be able to get out that list to help reinforce their self-belief.

Reputation — your greatest asset, and the hardest thing to repair

Ask yourself: would you do business with you? Many doors will open or close for you depending on your reputation, which will precede your presence every time. The people with whom you're doing business will have made it a priority to learn about you before you meet. What they discover — usually through the filter of other people — will either give you an edge or create early difficulties for you in your dealings with these new associates.

Ask yourself: would you do business with you?

Many doors will open or close for you depending on your reputation, which will precede your presence every time.

A 'firm but fair' reputation is the best one to have. What is yours? Does it need work? Try this exercise: write down five attributes that you'd like people to say you have. Stick that list in the front of your diary and refer to it often. Are you achieving your desired reputation?

I strongly believe that the presenter is more important than the presentation, the messenger more important than the message. If you have a good reputation, guard it with your life. However, if it has been tarnished in some way, now is the time to work on it. The only way to get it back on track is through action, not words. Don't tell me that you've changed—show me.

I remember dealing with an advertising agency that promised Boost the world but didn't deliver. In fact, it dumped us at another client's request. The ad agency rep claimed that he wasn't responsible, but he should have been honest about the process. If he'd kept me informed about what was happening, instead of blaming others when it was over, the situation wouldn't have been such a disaster. That rep is still trying to win me back over. I'm listening, but I'm cynical. He'd have to do (emphasis on *doing*, not talking) something amazing to win back my trust. All this is not to say that I don't believe in giving second chances. After all, everyone makes mistakes—just make sure you get it right the second time around.

Remember: every person and company has a reputation for something. It is the core of what you are. Jeff had a reputation for being a tough guy in radio and, even when he became a father and got a bit older and wiser (and a bit less tough in his core), he kept up his tough-guy behaviour because it suited his role at the time. I have worked with many businesses and suppliers over the years and have found it's usually no surprise why companies have the reputation that they do. What type of business it is and what type of reputation it's creating is usually highlighted when something goes wrong.

If it's a *great* business, managers and staff will go above and beyond to fix the problem, regardless of who is at fault. These types of businesses focus not on short-term losses but on the long-term reputation that they're developing—and so they thrive.

The other side is the type of business where, when things go wrong, managers and other staff put their heads in the sand and go into blame mode. This is a short-term view and often these types of businesses are the ones that don't survive—and the owners are left wondering what they did wrong.

Your business reputation is everything—it is why you will get repeat customers and referrals. A personal reputation is the same. I believe that my reputation is firm but fair—if you commit to me that something will be delivered by a certain date and you do not deliver it without any communication, I definitely have a reputation for not accepting this for too long.

Guard, or improve, your reputation with the following:

- Treat your reputation as an important part of your business arsenal. It will get you through doors—and also close them on you.

- If you've made a mistake in the past with someone, fix it. Win back this person's trust before a tarnished impression of you loses an important opportunity in the future.

Discipline—a daily battle to achieve

Self-discipline is the most common trait of great and successful leaders, while a lack of restraint can create big problems. Commit a few undisciplined acts in politics or business and soon you're being asked to drag yourself around the chat-show circuit.

Take alcohol, for example—just one alcohol-fuelled stupid instance at a work function and you could lose hard-won respect. As I've mentioned, one of my first jobs was working for an advertising agency as a media assistant. Back in the 1980s, the Christmas party where I worked was legendary. One year, a senior executive was absolutely blind drunk. He made a pass at anything in a skirt, threw a typewriter through a window and assaulted another client. He was fired the next day. The shame of it was that this guy was a good, solid executive who was simply a nasty drunk. If he'd had the discipline to respect that it was a work function, he could have had an amazing career in advertising.

In other words, if you drink and work, you're a bloody idiot! Nobody gets smarter after a few drinks. As a rule, I never have more than two drinks at a work function. Whether you're drinking with colleagues or suppliers, anything you say can and will be used against you the next day.

Set aside time each day for exercise. If you have the discipline to look after yourself, you'll feel better, look better and function better. As an added bonus, fit-looking people seem to garner greater respect from others, probably because others see that personal discipline will carry over into business.

Being self-disciplined doesn't mean being self-denying; it's not about working harder, it's about working smarter. Self-discipline is getting to your children's sports days, being home when you told your partner you would be, keeping appointments and being on time. Self-disciplined people aren't the ones in the office from dawn to midnight—they're organised enough to get their work done within a reasonable time frame.

Here's how to choose the right elements for self-discipline:

- In all aspects of life, control yourself before you influence others.

- If you are serious about career growth, say goodbye to alcohol and drugs and focus on your goals. You'll be amazed at how much more clearly you're able to view opportunities.

- You've heard it before—work smarter, not harder. Disciplined people aren't distracted during business hours, which means they get the job done in time to have a social life. How much time do you waste each day?

- Keep fit. Not only will you have more energy and be ready for any challenge, you'll evoke a great response in others.

Here's how to take your self-discipline up a notch:

- Do you know your weaknesses? List the top five character traits that you feel may hold you back or be your undoing. Keep this list in your diary and tackle one issue at a time.

- Are you a slave to your email inbox? Set aside an hour or two each day to organise and respond to your email, and stick to it. Don't let it distract you outside that designated time. If you do, you will only spend each day reacting to emails.

Listening skills—the reason we have two ears and one mouth

No-one learns anything while talking. Everyone has ears and using them to listen might be the most underrated quality of all. It goes hand in hand with asking questions, which is one of my favourite pastimes.

Are there people you admire? People you consider successful? If you get the chance, talk to them. If they're not immediately accessible, perhaps send an email to their corporate website or attend a public presentation they're giving.

Asking questions of successful people helps to remove the aura of achievement that surrounds them. You could ask them how they got started. (Usually you'll find the start point was a very basic opportunity, perhaps something available to many—only successful people have the foresight to grab opportunities with both hands.) You might ask how they find the best people, how they motivate their staff, and whether there is anything they'd do differently if they had their time again. See if they have one or two pieces of great advice they could share. Generally, most people like helping others—why not let them help you?

When I started out, there wasn't one particular person whose success I aspired to emulate, but there were two people who helped me.

Geoff Harris (co-founder of Flight Centre) had a profound effect in assisting Boost's growth. After he came on board, the business was able to go to the next level. Lesley Gillespie from Bakers Delight has also been very generous with her time and insight. She is an amazing woman who has been a great help to me.

At Boost and Retail Zoo, we're constantly looking for great talent on every level. A few years back, we were in search of a great board member—we felt that we needed more experience in international expansion on the board, and were recommended a man who had run a successful franchise business in the United States. We decided to try him as a board member. We paid for his first-class flight over from the US and put him up in a five-star hotel. We then put him on the road with our senior company store and franchise managers, so he could understand and learn about our business and get a feel for where he could contribute.

The feedback from our senior managers was horrific. They told us that all he did was talk—telling them how good he and his business were. He did not ask any questions on the financials, the product or the Australian market; he just talked and criticised. When I was told this, I initially thought that they may have been exaggerating a bit—until I got into the board meeting with him. The meeting opened and so did his mouth, and it just kept going. People were polite for a little while, but pretty soon I'd had enough and told him to shoosh. Yes—I said, 'Shoosh. That is enough.' He looked at me in shock and then told me his wife tells him the same thing—at which I suggested he listen to this wise woman.

When he was quiet enough that we could ask questions of him, he didn't have any answers. We asked him how the Australian model and his model compared, what the differences in the systems and processes were, how our labour rates compared with his and what he'd discovered during his time on the road. He did not have one answer to the questions that we put forward—because he hadn't cared to listen and find out or to gather enough knowledge on our business to be of any value. He was shocked and mortified that we did not add him as a board member.

As I said, you never learn anything from talking.

Improve your listening skills with the following:

- Listen to other people, and take notes. It's a great feeling to capture someone's full attention.

- If you can, create an opportunity to talk to someone you admire. Find out what worked for this person in the early days, and what didn't. Listen carefully to the advice. Although not everything this person says will be appropriate for your situation, much of it will transfer. Business is business, whether you are selling insurance, sofas or juices.

Here's how to really become a true listener:

- Make a conscious effort to ask more questions than you usually do and to say 50 per cent less for a day. Evaluate what you learn from that exercise.

- Don't assume you have all the answers, even when in a situation you're familiar with. And don't think you're the most interesting person in the room. Make it your goal to find out one new thing about another person each day.

Be solution-focused—try it, it will change your life

Albert Einstein purportedly once said, 'It's not that I'm so smart, it's just that I stay with problems longer.' You may not have all the answers to every problem you face. You just have to believe that you have the resourcefulness to *find* the solution to any problem—rather than asking your boss or mentor to come up with the answer.

If you're going to shine in the business world, you must be the person who presents the solution, not just the problem. I like it when a staff member comes to me and says, 'We have a problem and I think we should do this to solve it.' Like solving a puzzle, finding the right solution is a big reward in itself.

If you're going to shine in the business world, you must be the person who presents the solution, not just the problem.

We all have problems, but not everyone tries to come up with the answers. The employee who just sits there, looking like a puppy that needs rescuing and waiting for me or someone else to save the day, will not win Employee of the Month. In fact, if employees do that too often, I might start questioning if they're the right people for the job.

Think about it — don't you find that people tend to spend far too much time talking about the problem and not enough time finding the solution? People moving into 'protection' mode is one of my pet hates — when a problem occurs, they care more about not being blamed for it than about finding a solution and then putting a system in place so that the problem does not occur again.

In 2002 we were opening a store in Hornsby, New South Wales. The store was built in South Australia, shipped by truck and then put together in the shopping centre. Every store is specially designed for each site, so we can't just move one store to fit another site if there's a problem. The Hornsby store had cost us about $100 000 to build, and this was very early in the business when funds were at their tightest. Sharryn, my manager at the time, was on site making sure everybody was doing what they were supposed to. She called me at 10 pm on the night that the whole shop was meant to arrive and told me that the shopping centre had made a mistake and that they would not be able to get any services to the position, ever. If we could not open this store and had to write off $100 000 in shop fit, the business would be in a financially stressed position — one that we might not be able to recover from.

To her credit, Sharryn was on the phone to everyone and anyone for a solution. She managed to raise the centre manager and the construction manager for the site — and just would not take no for an answer. The store arrived and the so-called impossibility of getting services to the spot suddenly evaporated. We had services and all was good.

This is one of the biggest thought processes to learn in business — there is *always* a solution to every problem; you just have to stay at it longer. The person with the answers is you!

Here's how to stop looking at problems and start finding solutions:

- Believe in yourself and consult with others to confirm your thoughts.

- Knowledge, experience and research are the secrets to finding solutions. I have worked in every position at Boost Juice from the ground up. I use what I know about the business to come up with the answers; I then use the people around me to make sure they are the right answers.

- Don't fake it. If you're a manager and you profess to have all the answers, but really don't, take cover! People may listen while you're in the room but, as soon as you exit, the knives will be out. Instead, open up the problem for discussion and get everyone working together on a valid solution; your staff will respect you for it. However, the buck stops with you, so make sure you own the final decision.

Honesty (okay, not on *Survivor*)

Jonathan LaPaglia once wrote that lying on *Survivor* is like beach to the sand: it's part of the game and we all understand and expect to be lied to. To be honest it is so much fun being naughty and guiltlessly lying because lying in the real world does not get people very far and the benefit of lying is short-lived. Honesty is the bravest path you can take, and it is an essential element within a company's core integrity. It takes a brave person to be honest—in work and in life. Nobody likes to hurt another person's feelings, but most of us hate finding out that someone has been dishonest with us.

Often people don't mean to tell lies; instead, they filter the truth to justify their actions. This means that the picture you get is somewhat distorted, but the truth is in there—somewhere.

If you make a mistake, admit it. In most cases, trying to cover up an error will simply result in more problems. Trust is the first casualty of dishonesty. As a boss, I find that I get over someone's mistake very quickly if the responsible person owns up. We can then work together to find a solution. Once there's a question mark over someone's honesty, however, trust can take a long time to rebuild.

Honesty is the most refreshing part of business—a problem shared should lead to a problem solved.

Here's how to keep yourself honest:

- When you lie to someone, you're putting the relationship at risk. Is it worth it?

- The more honest you are in your business and personal dealings, the better you will sleep at night. Don't think for a moment you will be able to avoid your conscience constantly reiterating the guilt of having done the wrong thing. A clear conscience means a clear head—which means more room for new and exciting strategies.

- Most gains from being dishonest are short-lived. You can learn a valuable lesson from being honest about a mistake and then moving forward.

- Don't be afraid to admit you're wrong. I have seen general managers who are respected and loved by their staff because they are not scared to stand up and say, 'Sorry, I stuffed up!' Being human is endearing; being bravely honest reinforces the character of a true leader.

Power up your honesty with the following:

- You don't have to be brutal to be honest. By carefully listening and fully understanding the issues, you will be able to tell others the truth skilfully, in such a way that they are left grateful for your honesty. Try it.

- Are you truly honest with yourself? Do you let yourself not do things you said you would by making excuses? Do you ignore 'problems' within yourself rather than find solutions? Look at yourself honestly to discover if something is holding you back—and then find the solution to this problem.

Choosing your partners in crime

Financial success does not create emotional prosperity, so you need to make sure the person sharing your dreams is with you all the way. The truly rich life is a balanced one—unless you keep your work and family in harmony, your economic gains will be meaningless.

Having the right partner at home is vital. If your partner supports your dreams, your path will be a lot easier and, ultimately, success will come sooner.

The person you rely on may be a life partner, a friend or a family member. They may not necessarily agree with you, but this person must support you 100 per cent in your goals. The last thing you need is someone whispering negatives in your ear all the time.

Jeff and I are Yin and Yang — different people, but a perfect fit. We each have our own nuances and our own individual methods of operation, but we're highly effective as a team. He is the perfect complement to my style: an entrepreneur and the man with big ideas, but not always the attention to detail to make them reality. I am the planner and doer, the person who makes things happen. We often laugh that if it were just me in control of Boost, we'd have 10 amazing stores. If Jeff were in charge, we'd have a thousand — although they might have gone broke. His backup has been integral to my success.

When Riverside Private Equity bought into Boost in 2010, one of their primary concerns was having a husband–wife team running the company. It was their experience that such a team can quite often be a compromise of skills and expertise, so they gave us one of those long fandangled personality tests to see where we both sat. Based on the results of this test, we now have in perfect graph form what we knew intuitively — we are the perfect business couple. Every area I'm weak in, Jeff is strong in, and vice versa.

Your partner is critical in your journey. I see lots of couples where the wife is completely underrated and the roles are set in stone — the husband is the main breadwinner and the wife takes care of the family. This set-up all seems to go well in the early years, when the kids are super-needy, but it starts to crumble as the family evolves. Hubby is still mentally stimulated at work, the kids are in their teens, or older, and are more independent, but the wife is — hmmm — lost.

We all need a purpose, we all need to be challenged; however, in this situation what does the wife's purpose become? Women aren't just there for their husband's and children's needs.

Just as you should seek support from your partner, you should also encourage your partner to explore and fulfil as many of their skills and dreams as possible. These skills and dreams could be anything, but the earlier you start supporting your partner, the better your relationship will be over the long term. And hey! Just like our Boost story, you never know where you could end up. I can't imagine what my life would be like now if I had fallen in love with a man who wanted a stay-at-home wife, but I think it's unlikely I would still be with him.

I have become the best I can possibly be because I had a husband who encouraged me to have a crack at anything and believed in me to take on the world of retail.

Don't let your ideas be squashed for the sake of your family—you can fit everything in. And remember—happy wife (or husband), happy life.

Here are some components for perfect partners:

- To truly achieve your best, you need support from your partner or, even better, a partner who can contribute to your plan.

- Keep your partner informed and involved as your plans and dreams evolve.

- Look for a life partner who will bring out the best in you.

- Keep on the same path with your partner as much as you can.

Change how you think—yes, it can be done

Rome wasn't built in a day. Every cloud has a silver lining. If at first you don't succeed...

Looking on the bright side is not just for Pollyanna. Being positive is crucial to achieving success. Decide that you are going to be successful, and then be unfailingly upbeat in your pursuit of that goal. A firm decision makes you unstoppable—no 'maybe', 'could've' or 'should've' allowed.

You will get knockbacks along the way. Problems may arise from every corner. How do you remain positive in the face of constant negativity? By knowing there is a solution and that you will find it. If 10 people tell you your idea will not work, how do you keep believing that the eleventh person will love it? Well, it depends on who those first 10 people are. If Jeff or Geoff Harris were to disagree with me, I'd probably have to reconsider my position. If it were a person with no retail or business experience, I simply wouldn't listen. So many people have missed out on attaining financial freedom because they couldn't handle the knockbacks. If someone says no to you, don't close the book on the idea. It just means that the idea or request was not right for that person at that time.

Release the power of positivity with the following:

- Adopt a 'can-do' philosophy and resolve to chase your goal to the end.

- Don't listen to just anyone. Choose a few key people whose opinions and expertise you trust completely, and shut out everyone else.

- Don't take knockbacks personally. Meet challenges head on and learn from rejection. If you can understand the reason for a setback, next time you can find the path to a 'yes'.

Take your positivity to the next level with the following:

- Affirmations are a great tool for positive thinking. We all have an inner voice; get yours in a constructive frame of mind by choosing five uplifting sayings or quotes and repeating them to yourself daily. Perhaps have them stuck to your bathroom mirror and start each day by reciting them. Or have them on your phone or laptop as wallpaper—wherever you have them, just make sure that you see them every day.

- When negative thoughts creep in, stop them in their tracks and change them with positive thoughts. For example, *I'll never know how to do this* can become *If I ask the right questions, I can learn*, or *I will try to achieve it* can become *I will achieve it.*

Fighting negativity. You can do it!

Negativity is like a disease that can bring down the best and the brightest. The average person can have 200 negative thoughts every day. How exhausting! If positive thinking is one of your greatest weapons, negative thoughts can be your biggest threats. They will bring you down, no matter how good you are.

From my perspective, a service-oriented company is at the mercy of its staff's emotional moods. It's vital to recognise underachievers or dysfunctional personnel and either retrain or remove them. Some people simply do not like dealing with people. This doesn't mean they're bad, just that they shouldn't be in the service industry.

As the boss, my mood has a huge impact on my team, and it can dictate the atmosphere of the environment around me. Every person on the team can also have the same effect on those around them. One negative person in an office can upset the whole apple cart!

We all have bleak moments—we wouldn't be human if we didn't. But we also have the power to choose how we feel about the situations we encounter every day. Not every situation will be great, but you will see a lot more abundance and opportunity with the 'glass half full' way of thinking.

Throughout my journey I was driven by fear of failure, and in some ways it was a great motivator. This fear, for example, made me double- and triple-check everything I did to ensure that I did not miss anything. Fear kept my adrenaline at full speed, but there was a massive downside—you can manifest what you fear, simply because that's what you're focused on.

I'm not sure if I truly believe in books such as *The Secret*, but I do believe that if you have a positive mindset and you are looking for the good, then the good follows you. The more you focus on something (good or bad), the more likely it is that what you're focusing on is going to happen.

In the early days of Boost's success, I was a complete stress-head. Anything and everything would send me off, and everything was a drama. I was a terrible wife and mother and I was terrible to myself because I was so stressed. It got to a point when I stopped and realised that I actually hadn't eaten anything for three days. I was as thin as I have ever been (except for a month into *Survivor*) and, while my mind and body was all about making sure the business was a success, I was not living Boost's 'Love Life' philosophies, not even a bit. I was negative in my thoughts and my health.

This was a massive wake-up call, so I shipped myself off to a health retreat to get myself back on track. Once there, I came across a 'healer' (as you do at health retreats), who recommended I read *Conversations with God*. I'm not against religion, but it has never been something that I have wanted to be a part of. I do believe that I am quite spiritual, but I think spirituality comes from within, not from a church. The title of the book put me off straightaway, but I had nothing else to read so I gave it a go.

After the first few pages, I was ready to throw the book in the bin, because the author was basically saying that he was writing 'through God's words'. I persevered, however, and in the end I could not put the book down.

I have no idea whether or not the book really contained 'God's words', but I did like the messages. One key message was that you should not try to be better—you should just be better. Do not want to be a type of person, simply be that person. And the second key message for me was there is only love and fear—if you live in fear, you will manifest this; if you are grateful for what you have and are positive (or live for love), that will be what you manifest.

I do believe that books and people come into your life at different times for a reason, and this book (and the others in the series) did help me change the way I thought. I let go of fear and took more control over my stress, and that helped change the way I thought. Hundreds of books can tell you the same message. Forget about what you have or have not done in the past—all that matters is what you do now and into the future. Be grateful for what you have and don't focus on what you don't have.

Here's how to get rid of negativity in your life:

- Don't be a cynic. The best way to miss opportunities is to carry around thoughts like, *Nothing good ever happens to me.* Having a victim mentality will kill your chances of achieving financial freedom.

- Don't waste time overanalysing what other people might think of you. Assumptions, theirs and yours, are generally wrong anyway.

- Having an 'off' day? You can choose how you feel and react to things; it's all in your perspective.

11

THE POWER OF TEAM

People make or break your business, so this subject gets its own headline, because if you get this wrong, then your business will be one of the four of five businesses that fail in the first five years.

In my early years of business, my tips and lessons were all about hard work and dedication, and hiring the right people. But over time and after speaking to so many young entrepreneurs and highly successful people, my number one lesson has changed to this: simply marry well or choose the right partner. Do not get me wrong, if you are single or have married a dud, it does not mean you will not succeed. But I have come across so many people who have not had the support of their partners and it made the journey either so much harder or it simply failed. I look at my own journey and the support I had from my husband to be the best I could be. When I doubted myself, he was there to reassure me. When I came home stressed out of my mind, he was there to put it all in perspective. When we sold our family home, he was there to say we would make it work. He has always been there, supporting me and helping make me the best I could be. Without this support, we could not have achieved what we have. To have Jeff's honest feedback helps create the businesswoman that I am today.

But imagine the reverse: a partner who puts you down and says that it cannot be done; who says you're not capable because you have no proof that you can do it; who leaves you living in fear of losing everything. There is no way you could achieve or be the best you can be in this situation. Your greatest joy comes from hanging out with and marrying your best friend but the worst pain and stress comes from choosing the wrong partner. I have seen amazing men and women wanting to fulfil their passion but who have a constant battle with partners who may be well-meaning, but in the end stop their dreams. So this is my number one advice to my children. Pick your partner well.

Jeff and I are living proof of the power of a winning team. As a partnership, we're unstoppable. We complement each other's strengths and weaknesses and together we can achieve things that neither one of us would have achieved alone.

This is why it's so important to get the right team on board if you want to succeed in business. The right people are critical to the success of any business and, of course, this starts with you! But it will ultimately flow through to every choice you make about every person you bring into your business.

How do you find the right people? What do they look like? If I've discovered anything along my journey, I have learned that the most important thing employees can have is the right cultural fit. They have to fit in with your team. They must understand what it is that you're trying to do.

Secondly, they must have the right core fit. This is their attitudes: work ethic, ambition, self-motivation, passion, honesty and whether they're team players. Everything else is just mechanics—everything else you can teach them.

If you don't get the right cultural fit for the business, it just won't work. Unfortunately, in an interview situation, people will often tell you whatever they think you want to hear. It can be incredibly difficult to break down barriers to really get to the essence of the person.

Picking the right bunch

So, how do you sort the wheat from the chaff? We generally know within the first 60 seconds of an interview whether a person is going to fit in at Boost.

When choosing your team, it's important to ask the right questions. The culture at Boost and Retail Zoo is energetic, honest, passionate, sometimes funky, fun and always high performance. You can't fake those traits, so we don't need to ask an enormous number of questions to ascertain whether people will fit in—they either have it or they don't.

We have a rigorous selection process for employment at Boost's support centre and the 'cultural fit' interview is the last part of the process. Within this interview, we have specific questions that we ask candidates to answer and we look for specific traits within these answers.

The most important thing we are always looking for is someone who is solutions-based and 'can-do', not 'can't-do' or always needs help. Hire on type and train the rest. And, most importantly, fire fast when you get it wrong.

We look for people who fit the Boost culture, but it's also fair to say that the majority of employees in our head office are ambitious and self-motivated. This isn't a coincidence. At Boost, we're achieving twice as much as other franchisors in half the time; to keep up in this fast-paced environment, our employees regard their role as more than just a job. It may come as no surprise that many of our staff members are triathletes or are passionate about a particular sport; high achievers are drawn to Boost.

To keep attracting high achievers, we make sure that each candidate's core fit matches ours. We look for passion, ambition, self-motivation and drive. You can tell how much potential employees have of each of these traits by asking them about their 'achievements' in past roles, or in their personal life.

When recruiting for our stores, we always keep in mind that our customers are the most important people in our Boost world and that we believe we can create a customer experience like no other—and we know carefully choosing our in-store staff is the way to achieve this. We do not hire through traditional means, but, instead, mostly use an audition process. This is where we get about 100 young people in a room and we play games and do activities. People tend to relax and forget that they are going for a job when they're having fun, and this gives us a chance to see the true person. We are not just looking for fun, outgoing personalities; we are also looking for problem solvers and people with analytical skills—because the best teams are the ones that have a balance of personalities, not all one type.

Listen for the particular traits you value within your potential employees' answers. An obvious starting point is to say, 'Tell me about one of your greatest achievements.' You then just have to listen for the traits you value. If they match your 'core fit'—bingo! A follow-up question is, 'What do you wish to accomplish in the available position?' If the traits that are in your core fit exist within that candidate, it's generally easy to hear. We take hiring people very seriously at Boost, and sometimes an applicant may have to go through five interviews before we make a decision.

Keep in mind that honesty, integrity and high standards are harder to determine in an interview. For these you often have to go on instinct or past employers, or from the candidate's CV.

Firing the wrong 'uns

Even with our well thought out approach to corporate and store hiring, we do sometimes get it wrong at Boost. Some people will tell you what you want to hear to get the job. It can be difficult to get past that before it's too late. Alternatively, people's particular idiosyncrasies may only come to the fore once they're working in a team on a daily basis, or they simply may not 'get' what we want. I've learned that in these instances it is best to act quickly—not tomorrow, not next week, now! And act with a rigorous, not ruthless, philosophy. I received great advice once from a respected businessman, who said, 'Hire slowly; fire quickly!'

I've never been great at firing people, although I have gotten better with time. It's not an enjoyable process. Essentially, you're sitting down with people and telling them, for whatever reason, that you don't want them working for you anymore. This inevitably affects their ego and incites that terrible fear of wondering where their next job is. In short, it's a horrible thing to do. That being said, it's also a good thing to do. You'll find that in the long run it's probably the best thing for them as well. If you don't act quickly to remove the wrong people, you stand to lose the right ones. As a company with high standards, we have to uphold those standards, or other staff members start to wonder. Why put up with mediocrity?

In 2004, we had to make changes in the business. At the end of the year, we asked the heads of each department to assess their teams and decide who they wanted to take into 2005 with them. Unfortunately, a group of people didn't make the cut. Were they bad people? Far from it. They were just not right for Boost at that stage in its growth. As a leader, you must have courage, even when you hate doing what you know is the right thing for the business.

What are fireable offences? Obviously, dishonesty is a big one. Accountability is another. I do not want to hear about why your stuff-up is not your fault; if you try to make excuses, I will immediately lose an enormous amount of respect for you. I like people who agree that they've made a mistake and then tell me how they're going to fix it. Even better, I like people who bring a mistake to my attention, even if they know I'd never find out about it, and give me the solution. The kind of people who are not victims but take responsibility for what they do. As you may have gathered from reading chapter 2, I break this down into two types of people: VERB (Victim, Entitled, Rescued and Blame) and SOAR (Solutions, Ownership, Accountability and Responsibility). So I am looking for people who can SOAR.

Of course, an actual firing never really comes as a complete surprise. It's not like one minute you're telling staff members they're doing a great job and the next they're out the door. That doesn't happen. At Boost we follow the law to the utmost extent, ensuring that everyone gets a fair go. However, people have different levels of what they believe is acceptable.

You can't afford to have people who sit around twiddling their thumbs; you can't have one department drowning in work and another department leaving on the dot at 5 pm. Of course, as I've mentioned previously, staying late is not a badge of honour. But you do need people to deliver on what's required to get their job done. I don't enjoy letting people go, but it is a necessary part of my business. A situation will get worse if you don't do anything about it.

Leaders

I believe leaders may be born, but leadership is learned. What type of leader do you want to be?

My style of leadership has evolved through learning from my strengths and weaknesses. The business has evolved the same way. All leaders must evolve, but the fundamental philosophy should remain the same.

The role of a leader is to inspire extraordinary performances from ordinary people. If you're the boss, your level of enthusiasm will be reflected throughout your company. The more people you can influence daily, the more power you will gain.

How are you going to do this? Study how to be a greater leader. Define yourself, your values and your attributes. Play up your strong points and work on your weaker areas. Importantly, you must avoid the need to be liked. If you have a great personal life and feel secure within yourself, why should you desire affection from everyone? This need makes you vulnerable and weakens your decision-making ability; it has no place in building a successful business empire. Instead, you should aim to gain your employees' respect; you want them to respect you more than like you.

It's also essential to recognise leadership qualities in others, and these won't always be immediately apparent. That timid worker whom you've always perceived as slightly introverted may roar like the king of the jungle when put to the test. In the same way, someone who comes across as self-assured and competent may buckle under pressure.

People may try to tell you that one person cannot change the world. The reality is great leaders can—the great and evil things that have been done in the world always start with one person.

The role of a leader is to inspire extraordinary performances from ordinary people. If you're the boss, your level of enthusiasm will be reflected throughout your company. The more people you can influence daily, the more power you will gain.

Just think about all the great leaders out there, such as Mahatma Gandhi, President John F. Kennedy, Nelson Mandela, Martin Luther King Jr, Abraham Lincoln and the Dalai Lama—as well as leaders who people followed but who were far from great, such as Adolf Hitler, Attila the Hun and Joseph Stalin. What they all have in common is the passion and drive for what they believe in; their personalities are addictive, and people want to be them and be with them. They all had a very clear vision and would commit everything to achieve their vision.

The leader dictates the culture and, ultimately, the profit and growth of any business.

Boost your leadership skills with the following:

- Leadership is usually an innate ability, but your style of leadership can be chosen.

- Don't be the kind of leader you think you ought to be—be the best leader you can be. If you choose a style that's natural to who you are, you will be successful.

- Make decisions decisively after listening to all the facts; if you need to change your mind, make sure you communicate effectively.

- Communication is the best tool that you need to be a good leader.

Teamwork — business and sport … same same

I was fortunate to be the first female board member of the Hawthorn Football Club. I loved the years I worked with the club, and found the business of football fascinating. A key 'ah ha' moment for me was when we were discussing getting the right team to win a grand final, and how getting the right team balance leads to goals being scored. It was exactly the same formula as creating a winning team at Boost (and obviously a successful formula, as Hawthorn's three successive grand final wins can attest).

The 'recipe' for a winning football team was as follows: you need three to four superstars to start, and then you add your up-and-coming superstars. Next, sprinkle heavily with the solid team members (the ones who get their job done with no fanfare), while cautiously blending in the last group — those who need to move forward or move out.

The bottom line is this: a great team is a solid mix of different personalities, all working together to even out each other's weaknesses. A great team is healthily competitive, yet comfortable enough to truly celebrate each team member's individual wins. The right team can achieve the unachievable.

A good team mix could look like this:

- *The leader:* efficient, focused, ambitious, confident, honest, strong-willed and someone who can inspire. Leaders may, however, demonstrate little patience, a tendency towards bullying and a desire for personal success over team success.

- *The thinker:* analytical, concerned with detail, unassuming, precise, well organised, rational and a good listener. On the downside, thinkers may be perceived by others as aloof and negative — a killer vibe at the best of times!

- *The 'doer' or worker bee:* hard-working, patient and keen to get the job done without much fuss. Worker bees can, however, be easily manipulated.

- *The emotional creative:* social, energetic and competitive, but prone to the odd tantrum, especially under pressure, and may lack the necessary follow-through. In other words, creatives can be high maintenance if their astrological planets are not aligned!

A good team mix includes all elements from the preceding list, and manages to reduce the risk of any of the negative attributes associated with each element emerging.

When hiring new people at Boost, we know that the right person needs to fit into a team and the team needs to have a strong balance of various skills, so we hire to maintain this balance. However, we're also flexible enough to adjust the role to meet the candidate's skills.

Taking all of that into account, how do you pick the best team? It's important that you also recognise all the dominant traits in your team and balance these out—doing so will help to ease any frustration. You may have too many analytical types among your key personnel, for example, which means no-one will ever make a decision. On the other hand, if there are too many drivers and leader types, you're on a road that will be heavily paved with conflict.

If you're just starting out in your business (perhaps you haven't even got as far as creating a team yet), keep in mind that your first employee can really make or break the business. This time is when you are learning and focusing on growing the business, and confidence in your concept is what makes you grow. If our first employee had been a disaster, the growth of Boost Juice may have been very different, because timing in business is everything—at that stage of growing Boost Juice, we needed to quickly become the first option in the minds of the consumer. Luckily, we found Sharryn for our first employee.

Sharryn was the Australian speed-waterskiing champion—she had muscles on the muscles on her arms and, even though she could not be taller than five-foot-two, she could scare a man twice her size. Sharryn had never worked in retail before but she had the drive and the passion we were looking for in our new concept. She understood what we wanted to achieve and was passionate about achieving it.

Sharryn found herself running not one store but a number of stores very quickly. She moved from store manager to area manager and then to project manager, running the design and development team in opening new stores around Australia in just two years. She had no experience in this area either, but took on each challenge with enthusiasm. Sharryn salary-sacrificed her early wages to obtain a share of the business, which paid off handsomely many years later.

Fine-tune your team with the following:

- Develop a core team for your business that consists of four or five people who work well together and whom you trust. Under good leadership (yours) this group will become a cohesive unit, creating a synergy that will make your company or department unbeatable. Pay these four or five key players more than market rates, and make sure every single one of them is extraordinary.

- If you're not confident enough to conduct personality tests, consider hiring an expert to evaluate your staff.

- You are never going to get it right every time, but put systems in place to make sure you find out quickly.

People are your biggest asset ... and your biggest liability. Never settle for mediocrity.

Hiring people smarter than yourself

One thing Jeff believes he is very, very good at is picking people — as he says, 'I picked Janine as a wife, didn't I?'

For Jeff, the most important thing to focus on when picking people for your business is to hire people smarter than you. According to Jeff, 'once you absolutely and totally commit yourself to the idea that you are there to hire people smarter than you, and who will eventually take your role, the rest is easy.' In every company, only a small number of people can control whether the company is steered in the direction of success or failure — those people must be amazing.

Jeff says, 'My best-ever example of the "people" rule occurred during my time at Austereo. I had just started my radio executive career at Sea FM [on the Gold Coast in Queensland] as program director. I hired Guy Dobson, a bloke who is slightly left of centre, super-intelligent and has a real presence to him. We were both in our late twenties at the time. We

(continued)

Hiring people smarter than yourself (*cont'd*)

had a function on a boat and, over a beer, I asked him what he wanted to do in his professional radio life. He said he was going to be the best radio programmer in Australia. I laughed and said that was my goal too.

'Then I told him I was a year or two further down the track than him so if he helped me get there first, he could then take over the mantle. Done deal—from that day on, we looked after each other. He was outstanding, but his performance only made me look good too. We kept rising through the ranks until I got to 40 and stepped down from the head programming role in Australia to take a year off and then work with Janine. Guy was promoted into my role as group program director and then continued from there to take the role of CEO of Austereo. Total faith and total trust got us there.

'The truth is, I always end up having to figure out my next career step well before I'm ready to go because the people I surround myself with are so good that they put me out of a job. Your job as a leader is nothing more than clearing the path and helping your people have a clear run at hitting their marks.'

Relationships

If you want to learn about relationships, compete on *Survivor*. It does not matter how strong or fast you are—the best quality you can have is interpersonal skills. It is about being interested and interesting, making sure you listen and give that person 100 per cent of your attention when you are talking to them. When you are living on an island with no other distraction, relationships are everything—it was the people with the strongest relationships who actually made it to the end of the game, never the strongest physically.

Learning to manage the various relationships you have in business should be a fundamental part of your ongoing strategy.

On a day-to-day basis, I spend more time with my core staff members than I do with my family. Close bonds have grown between us over time; it's acknowledged that I would do anything for them, and vice versa. Together we have created and achieved amazing things, with plenty of hardship, stress and celebration along the way. In this kind of situation, you do develop a bond that's stronger than a mere employer–employee relationship. Not slipping over into complete friendship mode is a fine line, but one that I believe we now tread easily.

Being aware of this line is important, however, particularly for certain roles within your business. For example, the CEO of the company has plenty on his plate. He has hard calls to make every day. He said to me recently, 'I really don't have any friends in the company—as in mates I would socialise with.' And I thought, *Cool. That means you're doing your job right.*

The higher up the corporate ladder you go, the fewer 'mates' you will have in the office. Life and work are not a popularity contest—great people often have to make tough calls, and these calls are made tougher if a friend is involved. Sure, early in your working life, having workmates who are also friends can be super important, and going out and being able to live and breathe the day-to-day dramas of work is all part of it. However, climb higher and get older and, trust me, you need to keep them separate—doing so is rejuvenating for both aspects of your life.

These days, I have very little free time to spend with friends, so I make sure that those people I do see are the ones who make me laugh, allow me to feel good about myself, have my back and are honest. In business, you can be spoiled by the wealth of mental stimulation you receive from the people you meet. But in life, it is not what someone has or hasn't achieved that makes them interesting; it is who they are as a person. Friendships are vital to everyone. Nothing revitalises me more, or makes that bad day not so bad, than a good old belly laugh with trusted friends. Choose your friends wisely.

Here are some important elements for business and personal relationships:

- When you're passionate about your work, it's easy to neglect friends and family. Don't! There are only so many people in the world with whom you can have a close relationship—keep in touch. Good friends are the best tonic for bad times.

- The world is full of people who believe that the glass is half empty, that they are owed a living, that they are hard done by and that nothing is their fault. You do not need these high-maintenance people in your business, or your life. You owe it to the others around you to get rid of those negative influences.

- The best friendships are equal friendships. Look at your relationships: are they two-way streets? Do you feel good about yourself when you are with your friends? Make sure those around you bring out the best in you, and vice versa.

Protégés

Your job as a business owner or an executive in a business is to continue to grow strong people so that, eventually, you are out of a job. Start training your next-in-line now. Insecure businesspeople hire below them so they have control. This never works. Hiring the right people and training those people so that they can one day take over your role is critical to your success. Many insecure leaders hire people significantly weaker than themselves so they feel safe in their job. These leaders are limited and will ultimately fail. The great leaders are the ones that are always hiring people who can be their successor, and in truth make them look good.

Your job as a business owner or an executive in a business is to continue to grow strong people so that, eventually, you are out of a job. So start training your next-in-line now.

12

SHOW ME THE MONEY!

I see starting a business as a very maternal process. Just like you can't be half-pregnant, you can't be half-hearted about starting a business; you have to go all the way! A business can be very consuming, and it will take all your time, all your money and your entire soul to make it work. Sometimes the main thing that stands between the winners and losers is simply the ability to keep going. If you are serious about achieving success in your field, you can't just shove your business on the backburner every time you want to take an overseas holiday or when you've just had a big weekend and want to sleep in the next day. You've got to put your business first. It's your new baby and it needs you. Many people are simply not willing to make the necessary sacrifices to allow their business to succeed. For me, this type of obsessiveness was the only way to make the business work.

People are often attracted to the Branson and Zuckerberg success stories, and are keen to reach dizzying heights of success — along with all the trappings — as fast as possible. I have seen people who start a business with a flashy office, pay themselves a top wage and simply burn money. We're living in an era of 'NOW'. Everybody wants to have everything immediately and nobody wants to wait. But these businesses are often in the four out of five businesses that fail in the first five years. The reason for this failure is that businesses are hungry for cash and they need every cent to be spent on growth and on things that make a difference to the customer. When you prioritise your own needs, inevitably you run out of cash. Remember — many a good idea has failed due to lack of funding. New businesses are not about you and your needs; they are always about the business. So if you want the sports car and the corner office, maybe you would be better working for a big corporate. The reality of starting a business is likely that you will be living with your parents, or on the floor of your friend's apartment, working 100 hours a week.

Keep it in your pocket

If you're starting a business and living by the mantra, 'You have to spend money to make money'—you're wrong! This mentality will kill your business before it has a chance to grow. People look at Boost and they see an overnight success story, but nobody ever sees the hard slog behind that 'overnight' success. The reality is, I worked from my rental house for two years, didn't take a salary for three years and we didn't take a cent out of the business for five years! We even had to take the agonising risk of selling our family home in year two to fund growth—and that wasn't easy. There was no guarantee the gamble would pay off, but we were all in.

If you want to attract an investor into your business, the first thing you need to do is demonstrate that you are a good steward of your own finances. If you're not putting your business first and carefully measuring every dollar you spend to make sure you're maximising the value of that dollar, what faith can an investor have that you are going to show any greater respect for the funds they give you? If I sat down for a business meeting with a start-up company and saw the founders drive up in a flashy new car and hand me an expensive business card as they straighten a designer tie, I would start to question why they were meeting with me at all. If you can afford all that personal expenditure, why do you need an investor? The first place your investment should come from is yourself because if you're not serious enough about your business to sink your own hard-earned funds into it, why should anyone else be?

The smartest thing you can do as a new business owner is put your wallet away. Sit down and take a good look at your budget. When you really analyse it, you quickly start to realise how much money you simply waste on things you really don't need. How you feel about an 'essential' item right now is going to change over time. The more pressing your business needs become, the more it becomes like a hungry child. When that baby is crying for food and you have nothing to feed it, you're going to be thinking, *Why did I spend $150 getting my hair done? Why did I get the expensive wine? Why did I get takeaway four nights a week for the past six months?* Your whole priority system around spending will shift towards your business—as it should if you're serious about making it work. Suddenly a lot of the things you've been spending money on will make you sit back and think, *Really? This is what you wanted to do with the advertising budget this week?*

When I look back I think, sure I could have taken more holidays, spent more money on clothes, driven a nicer car—all those things. But if I hadn't sacrificed then, I wouldn't be part of the Boost phenomenon today. These are the sacrifices you'll have to weigh up if you're serious about going into business. Those small decisions about not taking holidays, going for weekends away, dining in fancy restaurants or spending money on nice clothes in those early years are the reason Boost is open in more countries than any other juice bar in the world, earning over $2 billion in global sales since inception. If I have one piece of financial advice for new businesses just starting out, it's this: put your wallet away. Your future self will thank you for it!

Attracting an investor

So, other than being smart with your budgeting, how can you catch the eye of an investor? You need to consider five critical things—and not all of them are about spreadsheets! Consider these points:

1. *Do your homework.* You should know your market well. Understand the competitive landscape and make sure there is actually a need for your product. One of the saddest moments I witnessed on *Shark Tank* was when we had to break it to a man, who had invested a huge amount of time, money and energy in developing a product, that the product actually had no market demand. He'd spent a fortune on something that nobody actually needed or wanted. I really felt for him as he walked away empty-handed and with his dreams crushed. He'd worked so hard for nothing. You also need to research and understand your customers. Meeting their need isn't enough—you also need to make sure your product is targeting them effectively and that they will like the way you present it.

2. *Know your numbers.* That means understanding every detail of your operation. How much does it cost to run? What are your overheads? How much does your product cost? What's your margin? Where can you make savings? Are there potential

economies of scale if you grow? How are you going to realise the necessary growth to ensure that your investor will get a return on the money they are putting in? How long will it take?

3. *Be smart about timing.* Is your business actually ready to scale up? Do you have the systems in place to manage sudden growth or will the whole operation fall over? What do you need to do to make your operation scalable? It could be something as simple as making sure you understand your payroll obligations if you need to hire staff. Do you know how much tax, superannuation and other entitlements you need to pay them? Is there a way you can outsource any aspect of your operation and is that practical? Are you investing in the right part of your business?

4. *Be passionate about your project.* I've often said that I'm at least as interested in the person as I am in the product when I invest. That's not to say I'll invest in something that doesn't interest me. There was more than one occasion on *Shark Tank* when I saw a really impressive pitch but had no interest in the product and so didn't invest. But a really great person can turn an average product into a fantastic business; whereas, even with a brilliant idea, the wrong person can turn it into a disaster. If you're really passionate about your idea, that reassures an investor that you will stick with your business through thick and thin because it's your baby. Someone who is in it for the cash will be easily disappointed and quickly look for an easier way to make money. Passion for the project is always a very attractive characteristic in a potential business partner.

5. *Think win–win.* While on *Shark Tank*, I had the opportunity to see dozens of pitches from hopeful businesspeople desperate to take their operation to the next level. Similar to the way I felt in the early days of Boost, they simply expected their business to be worth a fortune just because they had spent years on the project. But at the end of the day, the business is only worth what an investor believes they will get a return on. I often tell people in start-up businesses that they need to look at not only what they need, but also what the investor is looking for. The pitches that are flawed are the ones that only consider what they want without considering what they have to offer to the investor.

Connecting with investors

Starting a business involves many challenges, and one of the ones that makes many a good idea fail is lack of capital; or simply put—you run out of money. Young businesses are super hungry for cash, and you may need to look not only for money to start the business but also money to grow the business. As I said earlier in this chapter, you need to use every dollar in the business to return a profit, but sometimes no matter how careful you are, more is needed to grow. We sold our family home and I was lucky that we had a great deal of interest in the business so investors were not a problem in the early days. But getting the right investor was the challenge. At the start, when all I had was a document with the title of *Business Plan*, it was a bit different. These days there is crowdfunding and many business angels who are looking at investing. But even with these, potential investors would like to see some 'proof of concept'. What I mean by this is that the investor knows that the consumer wants the product. This may mean that you have to start on your own or with the support of your family, which in itself can be difficult. But you do need to get your business to a point where it is actually a business before you take it to the market.

Beware the 'Bank of Mum and Dad'

I have seen and heard some horrible examples of parents lending their kids money for their business and then, for whatever reason, it all goes horribly wrong and the parents are left in a terrible situation, often without their super or any financial security. Some parents are in a position to lend money and if they lose it, it's not the end of the world; other parents lend or guarantee their children with their super, or use the equity in their home as security to fund their children's dreams. This is, of course, completely understandable because these parents want to support their children in their dreams. But, if it doesn't work out, the parents can be left with nothing and some of them are retired so they are not in a position to make the money back.

Remember: four out of five businesses fail in the first five years, so if you approach your parents, understand what it would mean to them if the business does not succeed. And they should only lend you what they can afford to lose. This may all sound dark and depressing but I have seen the worst happen, and seeing a 60-year-old who has just lost their life savings on their children's dreams is no fun at all.

Are you ready for an investor?

Before you launch into seeking investors and setting up pitch meetings, ask yourself the following:

- Have I thoroughly researched my market and my customer? Have I proven that customers want my product?
- Do I know my business's finances inside out? Is my business scalable?
- Do I know what I have to offer an investor? When can the investor expect a return?

Mentors: you don't have to learn the hard way!

One thing I can't recommend highly enough is getting a mentor. Everybody needs guidance—yes, even you! As the journey of Boost continued and I was trying to manage the incredible growth, I discovered that there were things I didn't know. More correctly—everything I was doing was for the first time! Fortunately, I had help along the way, and still have a number of business mentors.

The mentor I mentioned earlier was Geoff Harris. We were the perfect pair: he received enormous joy out of teaching and I was a sponge that took everything in.

Geoff's message on culture fit was also loud and clear—in any meeting when we spoke about acquisition, the first topic that was discussed was always whether the possible acquisition was the right cultural fit for our business. One thing Geoff, Jeff and I agreed on was that we wanted to do business with people we liked and who had the same integrity and honesty in business that we had. If people did not get the tick, we would put a line through the business and move on.

I am thrilled to call this man my friend.

The others are people who may not be long-term mentors but who have been generous with their time and advice—people such as James Fitzgerald from Muffin Break, and Lesley Gillespie from Bakers Delight.

All these people have given me a wealth of invaluable knowledge. I've found that those who have been in business for many years are often very open about sharing their experience. It's refreshing when this happens, and it has always encouraged me to make sure I help other people where possible.

Is it any wonder that I firmly believe everyone should have a mentor? After all, nobody has all the answers all the time. Sometimes you just need help from someone who has been there before.

Nobody has all the answers all the time. Sometimes you just need help from someone who has been there before.

Ask someone you respect to be your mentor, your personal sounding board, but don't have too many expectations. As with all things, the timing must be right. The person you approach must be in the right circumstances to give you their time. Geoff Harris, for instance, was looking for an opportunity to help someone. Be incredibly respectful of that person's time. You should realise that you're encroaching upon this person's space. If the person you approach agrees to be your mentor, you must allow them to set up the means of communicating and amount of time given. Hopefully over time, your mentor may be happy to increase dealings with you. Always respect your mentor by following through on any advice provided.

If the person you admire doesn't have time for mentoring at the moment, look at other ways to study this person's success. Read about them, and read any books they may have recommended—there is always a lot to learn.

Keep in mind the following about mentors:

- A mentor can be an invaluable source of experience and wisdom. Sometimes the best thing a mentor can offer is a pair of objective ears.

- Be respectful in your approach if you're seeking someone's mentorship. Understand that a 'no' is probably not a rejection of you personally, but rather a reflection of the person's time constraints.

- If the person does agree to mentor you, don't expect too much in the beginning. Allow the relationship to develop over time. Also, prepare well for each meeting so you maximise your and your mentor's time.

- There are professional mentoring networks in place. By contacting one of these, you might be paired up with a suitable person who has decided they have the time to give something back.

- The best compliment you can give your mentor is to follow their advice — whether that is what book to read or what system worked for them. And *always* take notes.

Avoiding business pitfalls

When your business is becoming more established and successful, you may start to feel pretty pleased with yourself. The business may be on track, investors are taking an interest and life seems to be moving into the fast track, but beware: there are dangers lurking to trip you up. Whether you work in an office environment, a retail outlet or a work site, the traps can be the same, even if they wear different disguises. They're not always the most obvious problems — some of them may be considered assets under different circumstances. This section is all about knowing how to recognise problems — and overcome them.

Remember to harness your positive energy and there will be no such thing as an obstacle—it becomes just another lesson in business!

The following sections also outline what I have learned from being an employee and how to progress in your working life. One day (perhaps not too far away) you may be the business owner with many staff; in the meantime, learn as much as you can from being the best employee you can. Doing so will be so beneficial when you are the owner of the business.

Handling conflict

At Boost and Retail Zoo, we place an enormous emphasis on 'cultural fit' during employment interviews — and for good reason. It's not just to save us the hassle of employing a person who won't fit in; it's also to save that person the unhappiness of being a square peg in a round hole.

Dealing with people will always be your toughest challenge, and you need to make sure that you never settle for mediocrity. But sometimes you need to look in the mirror and ask yourself if you have provided all the tools and the right environments for staff to be successful. At times, we can inadvertently set someone up for failure by promoting them far too quickly.

Often the best outcome is to put yourself in the seat of the employee and realise that the best outcome for you both is that they are no longer working for you.

If you find yourself in an environment that isn't right for you, you will feel isolated. You'll never know what's going on, you'll never hear about the best opportunities for advancement and going to work will be an absolute chore. If you're the kind of person who likes peace and quiet, for example, and you find yourself in an open-plan office, full of creative types who like to bandy about ideas, you'll never be able to show your full potential.

If you're having a personality clash with one or two other people in a company of 100, well, that probably just makes you normal.

On the other hand, if you find it tough to name even one or two colleagues who you actually like, you probably need to take a hard look at your current position. Most people spend more time with their work colleagues than their family, so it is important that you enjoy your co-workers.

Solution

Find a job (or start a business) that suits your personality. Remember, if you're passionate about something, you'll be good at it! Passion can be quiet, but you need to be in a position where you feel confident about getting your point across. When you go for job interviews, ask a lot of questions about the 'culture' of the company—you want to make sure it's right for you.

Setting realistic expectations

When was the last time you woke up and thought, *I'm going to wow them at work today!* A lot of people trudge off to work (or even their own businesses) and sit down at their desks, prepared to do nothing more than what's necessary to get through the day. Low expectations like those could be killing your career or your business.

To get ahead you need to be more positive! I go to work every day determined to learn something new—and every day, I manage to do just that. There's always something you don't know.

If you've been killing time at your desk for a while now, you may find that other people have fallen into line with your low expectations. Has your boss given you any interesting new projects of late or suggested you attend a training course? If your answer is no, chances are your boss has noted your attitude. We get back the energy that we put out—if you're giving off bad vibes, nobody is going to go out of their way to give you opportunities.

Solution

It's time for an attitude change. Try surrounding yourself with positive mantras—write them down and put them where you'll see them in the morning.

Go to work with a smile on your face and a can-do attitude. If you lift the expectations of yourself, you'll find that others will too. If you look ready to receive more, you'll be given more. Yes, that might mean a heavier workload but, really, aren't you bored just sitting there watching the clock?

Also consider whether you're expecting too much too quickly. We live in a 'now' era. You only have to look at the spiralling credit card debt in our society to see that this is not a generation of people willing to wait patiently for things to happen. Too often young people sabotage their positions by demanding too much, too soon. Ask yourself if you're being realistic in your expectations. So you're not managing a department at 22—very few people are. Having said that, many of my employees may be considered young for the roles they hold, but they've worked very hard for their success.

I have never been a fan of those who believe they're entitled to things. Yet I've seen people take entry-level positions and then, within what feels like three minutes, demand pay rises or ask for promotions just because 'I have a degree', 'My friend gets x dollars' or 'I've been here three months'. I encourage ambition in my staff, but progression within a company has to be earned.

Some people manage to progress very quickly; for others it takes longer. If you feel you've been passed over several times, it may be time to speak to your boss, but overall you need to look at your career as a long-term prospect. Promotion may not happen overnight, but if you put in the hard yards and aim for respect from management and your colleagues, it will happen. Remember that respect and reputation are very difficult to earn and incredibly easy to lose. Don't forget about the big picture in a fit of pique about what's happening now.

Learning to say no

Do you find yourself saying yes to everything? A last-minute report needs doing, the photocopier needs fixing, you're loaded down with a big project, but you can't turn down the new recruit when she asks for help with her expense sheet. Every office has someone like you. Good old dependable you. The need to control (and 'fix') everything can be even stronger when it's your own business.

The trouble is that it's very difficult to remain dependable when you're being stretched in every direction. Sooner or later all those balls that you're juggling will start to fall—and you'll be too busy doing something else to catch them.

If you've found yourself in this role, you know wiggling out of it can be difficult, particularly if the word 'no' rarely passes your lips. You must assert yourself better. Taking up the slack in your office, department or business is not helping anyone—either someone else is letting you pull their weight or you're simply understaffed. Whatever the reason, your boss (or you) will never be able to manage resources if they can't get a clear picture of what's going on. It's time to stop working those incalculable hours; let others in the office stand on their own two feet. You don't have to be everything to everyone to be a valuable member of the team.

Solution

Learn how to say no. If you find that you're being piled up with work, under the assumption that you always find a way, it's time to sit down with your boss and discuss your deadlines. If your colleagues are taking advantage of your good nature, help them find the solutions for which they should be responsible by suggesting they put their own ideas together and discuss them when you get some time. There is always a way to let people down gently. If you don't start to do this, the only person heading for a fall is you.

Respecting others

You may call it being cool, or creative. Maybe you simply don't think about it at all. I'm talking about the little things that show a lack of respect—like being consistently late for work or not ready for meetings, throwing things together at the last minute, and passing the buck to others because you've got 'other things to do'.

What these things add up to is a big lack of respect for your colleagues—and never imagine for a second that they won't notice. They may not say anything at the time, but those slights are being filed away and will count against you in the future.

At Boost and Retail Zoo, we value respect immensely, but it has to be earned. It also has to be given. When you wander in late, fail to give 100 per cent or let others pick up your slack, you send a message to the rest of the team that they don't count. That doesn't make for a very happy workplace. I believe that happy teams make the best teams, and I do my best to weed out any negative influences. Any smart boss will do the same.

Solution

The old adage 'Do unto others as you would have them do unto you' has never held truer than in today's workplace. The best way to get ahead is to show your colleagues respect. They will not help you or make you look good unless you show them that you value their contributions. If one person performs badly, it lets down the whole team—don't be that person!

By the way, if you happen to be the person who's picking up the slack for someone—that is, having a heap of stuff dumped on you because your colleague 'doesn't have time', you're not doing yourself or your colleague any favours (refer to the preceding section).

Acting the part

You only need to read some of the chapters in this book to realise that I'm the last person who will ever judge people on their appearance. I don't believe that you need to present any other image than your own to be successful. But—yes, there's always a *but*—that's within reason.

Most workplaces or business types have a dress code and it makes sense to work within this code as best you can. Advertising agencies and other creative environments may seem to be freer with their fashion, but their unspoken rules of cool can be as set in stone as rules on attire in a corporate accountant's office.

Why would you bother with these rules? Two words: your comfort. If you're uncomfortable, you can't be at your best. If you stand out in your workplace or with investors, like Lindsay Lohan at an IBM convention, your fabulous ideas may never get the audience they truly deserve.

Which brings me to my next and most important point: actions speak louder than words. You can be the best talker in the office, full of amazing plans and strategies, but if you never get past the talking, you won't get far.

Solution

It can be difficult trying to sell your ideas and solutions to people who aren't looking past your belly-button piercing. You'll find it's easier if you take the time to work out the best way to express your personality within the boundaries that are acceptable in your workplace.

Also, once you've sold your ideas, don't forget the most important part of the equation — the follow-up. I don't want to hear about how well you can do something, or how quickly — show me. Very few people talk their way to the top (no matter how things may sometimes look). The truth is that solid hard work needs to follow up any burst of hot air.

Eliminating the fear

Whether you have a fear of failure or success, drop it! Everybody makes mistakes. There — the truth is out. Unfortunately, some people would rather not make any impact at all than risk making an error. You only need to watch an episode of a reality television show to see these people in action. In this situation, they're hoping to go unnoticed so they don't get voted out; however, even in this example you can see this tactic only works for so long. Soon the numbers get so few that those hiding in the shadows are forced into the spotlight.

In a work or investment environment, those people who never speak up, never volunteer and never commit will also never get ahead. They may get by without making waves for a while, but sooner or later their workmates will notice a certain void where that person should be. Nobody ever said that every member of a team has to be an extroverted leader. However, every member of a team does need to commit to the group. If you're too afraid of failure to even have a go, you create imbalance within the team.

Making an error will not be the end of your career or your business; write that down in your diary if you must. You need to step up to the plate and have a swing if you hope to hit a home run. The key to learning is having a go. As far as I'm concerned, learning something new every day is the key to a successful career. If you make a mistake, fine — own up to it and do your best to rectify it. I have more respect for people who do this than for those who skate through their working life, never really making an impact. After all, how can your boss see what you can really do if you never take a swing?

On the opposite side of the coin, many people seem frightened of the changes that success might bring to their lives. They feel they are imposters — that somehow the opportunities that have come their way were not really meant for them. They sit waiting for someone else to uncover the awful truth. I've seen talented staff who haven't gone for promotions because they're worried about ending up as the boss of one of their friends. Others are concerned about how their lives might change, and whether their partner will be able to handle their success. Many people go about their ordinary lives, ignoring great opportunities because they don't fit into the scheme of those ordinary lives. It's the few people willing to take a chance who find that success comes their way.

Solution

Face your fear. Try my 'worst-case scenario' approach: what's the absolute worst thing that might happen should you take a chance on success? Perhaps the partner you have right now won't make the jump with you — if that's the case, is that person really right for you? Perhaps you will end up your friend's boss — have you talked to them about it? How close is your friendship anyway? The point is this: can you live with the 'worst case'? Once you've identified the absolute worst that can happen, it usually just doesn't look as scary.

We can use a million reasons to convince ourselves that we shouldn't do something. We can use just one reason to convince ourselves we should: 'Why not?'

As for feeling like an imposter—and I've seen it with so many people—never underestimate the effort you put in, and accept that you deserve everything you've achieved. At times I think, *How did I get here? Me, who knew nothing about business?* Then I remember—*Oh yes, I'm here from a lot of bloody hard work!*

Face your fear … can you live with the 'worst case'? Once you've identified the absolute worst that can happen, it usually just doesn't look as scary.

Avoiding burnout

Not so long ago, I had days when I started to wonder what the hell I was doing. I'd spend 10 hours in the office, go home to spend a few hours with my family, then sit down at my computer to do another five hours' work. Of course, I'm not the only one who has worked that hard at some time in their life. The workplace is full of people spending way too much time in front of their computers and under fluorescent lights. Unfortunately, if we don't see the warning signs and put the brakes on in time, we will burn out. The fastest way to derail your career is to lose track of the importance of downtime.

Burnout is what happens when we don't get our work–life balance right. If you focus on just one area of your life, to the detriment of all else, it's no wonder things begin to go pear-shaped.

Stress can only be endured for so long. Long hours can only be tolerated for a little while. Being the first into the office and the last to go home will only get you brownie points with management for a short period. Once that wears off, they will simply begin to question your time-management skills.

In short, if you're beginning to feel that your workplace simply couldn't function without your presence, it's probably time to take a break. Holidays are a vital part of working life—we need them to refresh our minds and re-energise our bodies. Never underestimate the importance of taking a breather, and stopping to do nothing.

Solution

When was the last time you had a break—a proper one, without the laptop and the mobile phone? Trust me—the office will not fall apart in your absence. This may be a little deflating for the ego, but the health benefits will more than make up for it. When you return from your holiday, rested and rejuvenated, you'll be able to make that charge up the corporate ladder at full speed.

What I learned from my adventures

Here's what I've learned in my time so far with Retail Zoo:

- Having money in the bank does not make you happier; however, it does create the financial freedom to do what you want, not what you have to do.

- I look at businesses as children: in the early days, they need every part of you; as they grow and become more mature, they still need you but in different ways.

What does it take to succeed?

Some say, 'To succeed, you need money, a university education and to be really, really smart ...'

Bollocks! I started Boost Juice Bars on my own kitchen bench and have grown it to over $2 billion in global sales since inception—and I've never spent a day of my life at uni or a business school. Worse yet (according to advocates of a traditional pathway to success), I've never had a job I was qualified for.

What you really need to succeed is:

- to marry well—you need the support

- a huge care factor

- tenacity to keep at it, even when all looks lost

- to be a quick learner

- common sense

- impeccable integrity

- to work really, really hard.

Not having formal training to fall back on forces you to rely on your own innate abilities to achieve the unachievable.

13

THE GIANT LEAP

If, like with Boost, your domestic business has grown at such a pace that this country can't contain you and you're standing on the edge, staring into the great unknown of international expansion, then congratulations! You have achieved something truly amazing. Pause for a moment and celebrate your achievements. This is something we often forget to do in the crazy world that is running a business but you should always take time to appreciate how far you've come. But what if you're just starting out and part of your launch strategy is to break into a foreign market? When is the right time to launch into a new territory, how do you know your business is ready and how do you choose the right market?

Get ready to jump

Let me preface this section with the comment that every business is unique in the area of international expansion, but I think fundamentals can still be applied. The way that we have expanded overseas is by using a 'master franchise' model. You can enter overseas markets in this and other ways as follows:

- *Direct entry:* where you open your concept 100 per cent with your own money and you run the business as you do in your home market.

- *Using a distributor or licensing the product:* where you appoint a business to sell and market your product in that country and they take a percentage of the sales.

- *Internet-based sales:* where you run your business from Australia or elsewhere and you simply send your product overseas.

- *Master franchise:* where a business pays you an upfront fee and ongoing royalty and they incur the costs of growing the business in their market, and also get the profit from their enterprise. (For example, Domino's in the Australian market is under a master franchise agreement.)

I am sure there are a dozen more ways but, however you launch overseas, there will be positives and negatives.

Following are the top five things I learned from my experiences in expanding overseas:

1. *Arrogance leads to failure:* Just because your business works in your country doesn't mean that it will be successful in another. Take Starbucks, for example. Despite the overwhelming research that identified their coffee was not for Australians (because it was too weak and the Australian market had a sophisticated coffee palate), they still could not believe that Australians didn't like Starbucks coffee. They continued to invest, without adjusting their product or approach to meet the Australian market, and it failed. Boost's menu has differences in every country and we listen to the customers in each territory and adjust. McDonald's also learned their lesson in India. McDonald's first entered the Indian market in 1996, but they took millions of dollars of losses before adjusting to a menu that Indians loved. When they first entered India, they offered a Big Mac made with lamb called the Maharaja Mac but only one vegetarian option — when, as the managing director of McDonald's India has since admitted, half their customers were vegetarian. McDonald's India now also offers a local burger, the aloo tikki burger, which features a patty of spiced potatoes and peas. I think this is helping, but they have a long way to go.

2. *It's all about the people:* Currently our model is a master franchise model, which means the master franchisee pays an upfront fee and ongoing royalty to use the brand, systems and processes, and they then grow the business using their capital in their designated region. You will no doubt talk to very smart people on how to launch in each country and I am sure that some of the advice will be valuable. But all of our international wins and losses have been people based. We researched the big companies, who have multiple brands and lots of dollars and resources, but that option would

have meant we became one of many, and we would have lost what makes Boost special. We tried the passionate people who simply ran out of the money required to grow a brand. At the end of the day, you need both the focus and passion from a partner who understands you and your brand and has the financial resources. So what is the strategy for growing a master franchise successfully? The answer is to find the right person and get to know them over time and, if you are happy that they have the right attitude, funds and infrastructure, you have a higher chance of success.

3. *It's also all about relationships:* As with all good business relations, communication and relationships are keys to success. We have a strong team of people dedicated to the international part of our business, and they have a solid communication system in place to ensure they communicate and work closely with our international partners. If you do not communicate with people, what they make up in their head is *always* 10 times worse than the reality. For example, my son Riley called me to say he had some bad news he wanted to tell me when he got home. I immediately went to the worst-case scenarios: he has got a girl pregnant; he's had a serious accident; he is in trouble with the police; he has a drug problem ... By the time he got home, I was a mess. In the end, his bike had been stolen from school.

4. *Research is key:* Research is critical before moving into markets. For example, our market at Boost in Australia is mostly a 'grab and go' one, but when we researched the Asian market, we discovered they are more of a 'buy and sit' market. Every market has its nuances, and you need to know what they are before you invest heavily into those markets. Some countries are difficult to get money out of— for example, South Africa. Trademark laws are different in every country. Franchising laws are very different—in some countries, you need to be approved to be a franchisor, and other countries have very few rules to follow. The most important research you should be doing here and overseas is always (did I say *always?*) talk to your customers and ask them about your product, price and promotions. Whatever the differences, it is best to know before you enter into the market—rather than when you have already invested. The government body Austrade is also a great resource—it exists solely to help you grow your business overseas. And the Export

Market Development Grants scheme (EMDG) is also well worth investigating if you are looking at exporting your business or product.

5. *You need to understand what you are prepared to give to achieve this goal:* We decided as a business that we would start to research the US market. Jeff and I flew to the United States and stayed there to see how we could make this work. We actually stayed so long doing the research that I gave birth to my fourth child there. After a full review, we decided that our concept should work. We met with all of our competitors and reviewed our options: do we acquire an existing juice bar and convert, for example, or do we start fresh? We did the numbers and looked at every shopping centre in California, and eventually made an offer on a great site in Century City in Los Angeles. We were excited with the prospect of growing the brand into the US market. What we forgot to ask ourselves was, what do we want as people, not as businesspeople? We knew on paper what to do, but we realised the only way we believed it would be successful was if Jeff and I moved our family to the US for at least a year to really drive this business forward. The truth was that neither of us wanted to live in the US. We didn't want to uproot the kids. So, we were torn between wanting to expand to the US and our personal needs. In the end, the site was given to another brand, which gave us some time to review how we could make this work. It was all very well to have the idea, and the funds, but we also knew if we or other key executives were taken out of the Australian market at that stage, it may affect the core business. The plan was to regroup and work at growing a team to be able to grow overseas. Timing can be everything, as just after this the US went into meltdown with the global financial crisis (GFC) and so any plans of going into the US were put on hold. The US is still a market we will enter, but we will do so when we are ready.

Learn to love the boring stuff

I personally do not think I am an entrepreneur in the true sense; in fact, true entrepreneurs make terrible businesspeople. Yes, they are passionate, work hard and are obsessed with their product or dream, but they get so caught up in the logo colours, the pretty product and all the sexy stuff in business that they forget some of the most fundamental operations of their business. For most entrepreneurs this is the 'boring stuff': accounting, policies, contracts, trademarks, patents, and so on. I have seen dozens of failed entrepreneurs who, just when the business starts to struggle from lack of love of the 'boring stuff', start following another bright light, then tend not to stick to the next idea long enough to make it work.

Still loving life

Like any baby, a business eventually grows up and becomes more independent, and Boost is no exception. As we began to expand into more overseas territories and our team grew stronger and more experienced, I began to realise, *hey, I can take a holiday and the sky doesn't fall in. And my phone is ringing less often at strange times of the day and night!* That's when I began to realise that the great team we'd hired was doing exactly what we hired them to do and our little business was getting to be all grown up. But when you've been in the thick of the action for so long it can be hard to switch off. That's when I realised it had been quite a while since I properly took care of me.

Ever feel like a mouse on a wheel? You know, running and running and going nowhere...fast? Sometimes you need to get off that wheel, for the sake of your mental and physical health. As entrepreneurs, we are so driven by our own passion for our project that we can be our own worst enemies. This section is all about ensuring you're happy with your work–life balance, and taking care of you—regardless of what stage of the journey you're on.

There's more to life

Do you feel like there just never seems to be enough time in the day to fit in everything you want to get done? If you're anything like me—a parent, with a business to run or a job you're passionate about, and a partner whom you love to spend time with—the days probably fly by. Sometimes the pace of my life is enough to make me wonder whether somebody has actually dropped an hour or two out of the standard 24-hour day without telling me.

In the early days, you give everything to your business to ensure it succeeds. But as the business matures and you start to get more experience and more people in the business, you need to start letting go of certain areas. Often entrepreneurs are 'Jacks of all trades'—and you have to be—but as you grow, you can get specialists into the business to do the job 10 times better than you can do it yourself. Your plan should always be to do yourself out of a job. Although this may take years, a great business is one you can go away from and know it will still run smoothly. This is what we all need to aim for to achieve that elusive work–life balance.

Work–life balance is something that's talked about a lot these days. But what does it mean? To me, there is just life, all mixed up together with the balance part. It is all about finding happiness and contentment; getting enormous stimulation from my work, yet being equally happy to sit down and play Monopoly with my son for two hours. Sometimes I do find it hard to drag myself away from work—when you're really passionate about your job, it can be all-encompassing—but I'm getting better. I'm learning to switch myself off from the office and enjoy the other aspects of my life as well. I think that we will all be better wives, husbands, mothers, fathers, employees, leaders and friends if we find that happy medium.

Work–life balance is about prioritising what's important to you, and having equal space in your life for your job and your family. Unfortunately, a lot of employers only pay lip-service to flexible work hours and 'family time'. The reality is that you get paid to do a job and the job has to get done. Having said that, work–life balance is becoming recognised as an important strategy in creating a healthy corporate culture. The best companies are certainly making great steps in that direction and they're finding great improvements in productivity in the process.

There is no point in creating success, if you are not healthy and happy enough to enjoy it.

Prioritise

You will never get what you want if you don't know what that is.

It's time to stop seeing work or your business as something that finances the rest of your life, and start thinking about doing what you love and making money from it. I know I've reiterated the idea of passion several times in this book, but that's because I feel so ... well ... passionately about it. If you're still not sure how to define your goals and dreams, find a mentor to help.

My kids are my priority, but I believe that children are in *your* life; you're not in theirs. Admittedly, this gets easier as kids get older. I work killer hours, there's no doubt, but I fit them in around quality time with my children. When I'm at home with them in the evening, it's their time. We do normal things such as reading and watching television until they have to go to bed. Then it's my time again, the laptop comes out and I do what I need to do. Yes, it's a long day, but I wouldn't do it if I didn't love it.

Of course, I would like to say that there's no way I ever compromised family life by letting my work take over completely but, honestly, work did sometimes take a front and centre position. None of us is perfect and life forever is a balance — trying to keep all the plates spinning in the air at the same time does not always work.

I have taken my children to school when no school is on, and they have gone in the wrong uniform many times, but mostly I did get it right — and, hey, that is life.

It takes two

Jeff and I are both passionately involved in Boost and Retail Zoo. Do we ever see each other? Do we ever talk about anything other than business? The answers are yes and yes. I must admit we do have corporate meetings over dinner, but both of us are aware of the importance of letting each other switch off. We understand when one of us arrives home from work and simply doesn't want to talk about business. We also make time to go away together. We have a good, open relationship (which is vital) and enormous respect for each other. Even with that kind of partnership as a base, you will have your ups and downs; Jeff and I always talk through our differences — sometimes at a loud volume.

I am very lucky that, 25 years on, I am madly in love with the man I married. Like with any marriage, he drives me mad and at times I could throw him under a bus, but that only lasts an hour or so and then we are laughing again.

Get help

Who said that you have to do everything? Women in particular suffer badly from the 'I must' syndrome: 'I must put in a full day's work, organise the family, clean the bathroom, collect the dry cleaning, bake for the school fete' and so on. Get over it! Terrific people are working hard to make a living doing those things you don't want to do. Let them. Whether it's a cleaner, a gardener or a caterer you need, call in the professionals and save your energy for chasing your goals—and do not feel guilty. A happy woman is a happy mother and wife, and if we are happy we are so much better at both.

Work out how much you need

There's a tendency today for us all to be working at making as much money as possible—without really knowing how much we need.

You don't have to curtail your financial ambitions, but if it's money that's driving your workaholic tendencies, it might help to sit down and cost your ultimate lifestyle. Once it's written down, you may find you don't need as much cash as you think. Or you may find the motivation you need to start overachieving!

Enjoy extracurricular activities

It is healthy to have a hobby or social activity outside of work that helps you relax and forget the problems of the day. I feel very strongly about this. I do yoga five days a week, and this is a time where I can focus on nothing else but me. Whether it's dinner with your mates, a visit to the gym or whatever—don't get too busy for something that helps you cope with life's pressures. You can always find time for the things that are really important, so make this important.

★★★

Here's how to really focus on improving your work–life balance:

- Know that at times in your life your work–life balance will be out of whack, and that is okay. Do the best you can to juggle and create coping mechanisms along the way. But, in order to achieve, you will very likely need to have the balance that is not ideal.

- Find a weekly or regular activity you enjoy—join a running club or organise a regular get-together with friends. Or perhaps join a book club—not everything has to be related to business.

- Create some boundaries between your work and home life, and put some emphasis back on health, social life and relationships.

- Clean up your desk. You know where everything is, but do you really need everything? It sounds simple, but you will feel much better when you're not working in chaos!

- Hire a great PA and support people such as cleaners so you actually do have time to do the things you love.

Taking care of yourself and your health

I am over 50 and I have never been fitter and healthier. I believe taking care of you is taking care of business. You can't win in business, or in life, unless you look after yourself first. When you're chasing a goal it can be easy to overlook simple things such as sleeping, exercising and eating right. All I can say is don't. Working around the clock makes you inefficient and unfocused. Sitting on your backside all day makes you sluggish and, let's face it, overweight. A diet of caffeine and fast food will leave you low in energy and not looking or feeling your best. It does not matter how financially successful you are; if you do not have your health, you have nothing.

As I've said before, I'm passionate about eating right and I don't miss my yoga for anything. I also do my best to get a decent sleep every night. But I am human—I understand what it's like to be so stressed that you physically can't eat. The key is balance.

We all have heard the saying, 'You are what you eat—and drink'. Boost defines 'eating for success' as eating naturally, and avoiding artificial colours, flavours and preservatives. The emphasis is on fresh and nutritious. It's a theme repeated in one of my favourite books on the topic: *Laugh with Health*, by Manfred Urs Koch, which focuses on health, diet and natural foods. Of course, I'm not suggesting you suddenly adopt a macrobiotic diet—it's more about doing what you can do within the confines of your busy life.

What do I do? I eat as much unprocessed food as possible—I eat a lot of fruit and veggies. If I pick up a packet of food and the ingredients label has numbers and words I cannot pronounce, then to me this is not food. Yes, I have a smoothie or juice (sometimes both) every morning. I'm a big fan of all our juices; the simple ginger, carrot and apple juice is my 'go to' juice. Lunch is usually a big sandwich packed with chicken and salad. We try not to eat a big meal at night, because the body simply cannot digest the food quickly enough before bed and, if I eat anything too big, I find myself tossing and turning. So our big meal is during the day and we go light at night. (The kids are different—they need the calories and the carbs to grow into healthy, strong adults—so we tend to cook a meal for them and something light for Jeff and myself.)

This is how I eat most of the time; however, life sometimes gets in the way and I find myself not eating the way I should. When this happens, I cannot sleep and feel and look lousy—and I know I need to get myself back on the health wagon. I could not do what I do if I did not eat healthily.

I'm very conscious that what I put into my body is the only fuel it has to run on. Given the pace of my life, I do my best to make sure it's efficient. I could always do better, but I do what I can with what I've got. I'm lucky that juices and smoothies are such a fast, nutritionally packed option! (I know it sounds like a sell job, but it really is true.)

The power of fresh juice!

Ask me what my secret weapon is and you'll only get one answer: juice, of course! Why am I so passionate about juices and smoothies? Because they work! There are no short cuts to good health, but there are steps you can take to help you on the journey. If you're anything like me, there aren't enough hours in the day to plan and cook the right meals to fit five serves of vegetables and two serves of fruit into your diet every day. That's before you even consider the raft of vitamins and minerals that are essential to efficiently run the human body, and the veritable mountain of food you need to get through to ensure you get your quota of each.

Every year Boost Juice uses over 3 million bananas, 6 million oranges, 5 million apples, 8 million carrots, 2 million sticks of celery, 600 000 pineapples, 2000 tonnes of watermelon, 20 million strawberries, 1 million mangoes, 21 million raspberries, 49 million blueberries and 3 million passionfruit in our smoothies and juices. (These figures are based on 2014 Boost statistics.) That's an enormous amount of fresh fruit and vegetables! A glass of juice can be considered an excellent snack—it's healthy and it will fill you up. An average glass of orange juice contains about five oranges—and there is no doubt that it is a great way to mainline a cocktail of vitamins in minutes. Imagine sitting down to eat five oranges. You'd need a whole soccer team to get through them! It always puzzles me that people only turn to fresh food when they have a health problem. Why wait?

Fruit and vegetables are an excellent source of vitamins, minerals, phytochemicals and antioxidants, which are all essential for a healthy body. Vitamins are organic compounds, and are classified as either fat-soluble (such as vitamins A, D, E and K) or water-soluble (the B-group vitamins and vitamin C). Fat-soluble vitamins are stored in body fat while water-soluble vitamins are carried in the blood and excreted in urine so are needed in small, frequent doses.

There are 13 recognised vitamins, each with a special role to play in the body. They do everything from regulating your metabolism (how food is digested, absorbed and used within the body) and helping to produce energy, to assisting with the growth and repair of body cells. Apples, bananas, beetroot, carrots, celery, ginger, lemons, mint, oranges, pineapples, raspberries, strawberries and watermelons are all good sources of vitamins. Conveniently, they also combine well in juices!

Minerals are pure, inorganic elements required in small amounts for good health and growth. Think zinc, magnesium, potassium and other tasty-sounding substances. Minerals form the bone structure of the body, play an important role in the chemical reactions that keep your body going, regulate water balance, and assist in controlling nervous responses and muscle contractions. There are 16 minerals considered essential to our health. While it can be difficult for the body to absorb minerals, it's important not to over-consume them (for example, in concentrated tablets) because they can be toxic in high levels. Good sources of minerals include bananas, beetroot, carrots, celery, ginger, lemons, mint, oranges, pineapples, raspberries and watermelons.

Phytochemicals are plant chemicals that contain properties that may aid in disease prevention. There are thought to be more than 900 different phytochemicals in the foods we eat, and it is believed that they tend to act together, rather than in isolation. Phytochemicals are found in tomatoes, spinach and other leafy greens. They can also be found in apples, carrots, citrus fruits (such as oranges and lemons), ginger, mint and watermelons; there can be dozens of them occurring in any one serve of these foods.

Finally, antioxidants — a major group of phytochemicals — act as a bodyguard, limiting the activity of free radicals in the body. They include vitamins A, C and E, selenium and the carotenoids. Freshly squeezed juice is one of the optimum ways to reap the benefits of all the goodness in fruit and veggies. For even more nutritional benefits, try including some of the ingredients we use in Boost's 'boosters'. There are, of course, natural sources for all of them, but when you can get them all together in one power-packed cocktail, it makes sense. (Remember — all our supplements comply with the guidelines from Food Standards Australia New Zealand.)

If you do only four things to help keep your health on track, make them these:

- Drink more water—very few people drink enough of the liquid gold. Always have a bottle or glass nearby and use it.

- Eat as much natural wholefood as possible and eliminate highly processed foods from your diet.

- Do not eat too late; it is terrible to eat a big meal and then go straight to bed.

- Do not beat yourself up if you have eaten poorly in a day. There is always tomorrow. As long as poor eating is the exception not the rule, you will be fine.

The secret

So how did I get here? What's the secret to it all? There isn't one. I believe that my personal success is due to a combination of many factors: naivety, my certainty that there is a solution to everything, and the great people who surround me. I now believe in myself and, if I'm given a challenge, I don't question that belief.

I now believe in myself and, if I'm given a challenge, I don't question that belief.

I believe Boost has been such a phenomenon because it's a great product, we are always, always honest and it's marketed well; every store acts as a billboard for our brand. Beyond that is my unshakeable faith in the necessity of doing the right thing, of having the right people and looking after them, and of understanding your customers and giving them what they want.

I'm passionate about health and I want to do everything I can to help counter the terrible toll that the fast-food lifestyle is having on our society—particularly on our children. The desire for a healthy alternative for my own kids was a large part of my initial interest in juice bars; that desire hasn't wavered. Passion can't be faked. Our sincerity is one of the reasons our customers have taken to Boost Juice.

Now what?

What happens when you climb your Everest? Does the journey ever actually end? I would say no. We humans need a purpose. Going on the Boost journey was not only a purpose, it was an obsession and I had to dedicate everything I had to it to make it work. There was no life balance. There was no catching up with friends. At times, there were no dinners at night, because I was too tired—and also needed to do some important job that needed finishing. There was no holiday where I could go away and not think about work. In the early days there was just Boost. We all talk about work–life balance, but there is seriously no such thing when starting a business.

What do you do once you have climbed your Everest? You try to create balance. I could not give up work and I would not want to, because I love how problem-solving makes me feel. I love the challenge. I even like the negatives because this is when you go into problem-solving mode. The big difference is, this time, I have learned many, many lessons—and I know there are many more to go—and I am now more prepared for whatever life throws at me.

What drove me in the early days was fear. Fear of failure; fear of losing everything; fear that people would actually find out that I was winging it and trying to work it out along the way (what do they say—'fake it until you make it'?), while inside I was not as confident as I appeared to be. Now I have a great balance and I'm a better person because of it. I have a healthier outlook and actually now have friends that I go out for dinner with and hang out with.

Life is what you make of it. We all have stuff that goes pear-shaped and things we would prefer not to have happened, but I would not change a thing, because it's made me the person I am today. And I quite like her. She is not perfect, she still cannot spell and makes words up, she is flawed but is happy in her flaws. She is me.

The last words

My philosophy about the importance of sharing knowledge and experience is the reason I have written this book and I hope you've enjoyed reading it. Most of all I hope I have inspired you to follow your dreams. There's nothing special about me. I did not complete year 12, did not go to university and I'm a shocking speller. I'm just a girl from the suburbs—and if I can do it, so can you! Enjoy the journey as much as the results ... and most importantly, *love life*.

Index

Printed in Australia
17 Jun 2024
LP032063